Faith and Practice

The Seed, or Grace of God, is small in its first Appearance, even as the Morning Light; but as it is given Heed to, and obeyed, it will increase in Brightness, till it shine in the Soul, like the Sun in the Firmament at its noonday Height.
~ Elizabeth Bathurst

Faith and Practice

Northern Yearly Meeting
of the
Religious Society of Friends

Copyright © 2017
Northern Yearly Meeting of the Religious Society of Friends
All rights reserved.
ISBN: 978-0-9987288-0-3 (paperback)
978-0-9987288-2-7 (hardcover)
978-0-9987288-1-0 (Epub)
Composition by Clark Kenyon

First Edition

Permissions

Acknowledgement is gratefully made for special permission received for inclusion of original work from these individuals, as follows (with date or year permission was given):

Nancy Peterson, April 4, 2014, for poem on page 61.

Hannah Hutchinson, original drawing frontispiece, February 29, 2016. Elizabeth Bathurst, "Truth's Vindication," London, printed by Mary Hinde, 1773. https://books.google.com/books/reader?id=ZOReAAAAcAAJ&printsec=frontcover&output=reader&pg=GBS.PA119.

Frances I. Taber, May 22, 2005, Simplicity chapter. Material published in 2009—Pendle Hill pamphlet # 400.

Sheila Thomas, 1999, Integrity chapter.

Patty Weerts, 1999, Integrity chapter.

Rosalie Wahl, 2002, Structure and Function chapter.

Philadelphia Yearly Meeting, Covenant on Education, July 1999. by Tom Hoopes, PYM Coordinator of Education, September 22, 2000.

From the Favorite Quotes chapter:

David Langworthy, *Prayer for Simplicity, Among Friends: Poems.* Permission given by his daughters, Sara Langworthy, Leah Langby, and Toni Langree, June 1, 2016.

Francis Hole, "Original Psalm, inspired by Psalm 19," permission given by his daughter, Sarah Hole, June 30, 2016.

John Kraft, January 1, 2007.

Raquel Wood, story "Aw, Shut-Up," June 17, 2016, as printed in 10 Year History of NYM, 1985. Rich Van Dellen, June 10, 2016.

Table of Contents

Permissions / 5
Acknowledgments / 9
FAITH / 11
    Queries – An Introduction / 13
    Spiritual Beliefs of Friends in Northern Yearly
        Meeting / 15
    Care for the Earth / 21
    Integrity / 31
    Peace / 35
    Equality / 41
    Simplicity / 47
    Community / 51
PRACTICE / 63
    Meeting for Worship / 65
    Decision Making / 71
    Yearly Meeting Structure and Function / 79
    Membership / 89
    Marriage / 97
    Spiritual Nurture of Children within the Meeting
        Community / 107
    Education / 113
    Preparing for Death / 119
HISTORY / 127
    A Brief History of Quakerism / 129
    A Brief History of the Peace Testimony / 143
    The Early History of Northern Yearly Meeting / 151
RESOURCES / 167
    Quaker Quotes / 169
    Quaker Resources / 181
    Appendices / 189
    Index / 207

FAITH AND PRACTICE

Acknowledgments

Appreciation is expressed to all the individuals who served on the committee, and all the individuals and groups who wrote, read, and commented on the chapters, provided information, sections, quotes, and suggestions over the twenty-two years of development of this Faith and Practice

We cherish the memory of dear Friends who have contributed much to the life of our yearly meeting and who have passed on during our first forty years, including Nancy Peterson, whose poem reprinted from the Northern Yearly Meeting Newsletter, January 2011, appears with permission.

This Faith and Practice is offered as a consultative and imperfect document about being Quaker in the upper Midwest of the United States in 2016. It is offered as the current understanding of our witness, according to the date each chapter was approved by the yearly meeting. We do know that words only partially convey this understanding.

We also have experienced what a dynamic, yet imperfect document this is. Our yearly meeting may choose, at any time, to review and rewrite or delete any of these chapters, as we continue in loving community.

The Faith and Practice Committee
of
Northern Yearly Meeting
March 2016

Faith and Practice

FAITH

The central purpose of our disciplines of simplicity and plainness is to clear a space, to...catch a glimpse of the Holy Stillness that lives before and beyond the busyness of both our inward and outward lives. It is in worship that we bring ourselves to the threshold of that Stillness and offer ourselves to the Grace that draws us down into The Seed of Life where we come to know the place before words, before forms, before outward witness....It is this Life that gathers us, that creates, and sustains our community...

Daniel O. Snyder, *Quaker Witness As Sacrament,* Pendle Hill Pamphlet #397. (Wallingford, PA: Pendle Hill, 2008), pp. 18–19.

Faith and Practice

Queries – An Introduction

Historically the queries came from the yearly meetings as both a tool for discipline and to gather statistics and information about the local meetings. The disciplinary queries asked questions about behavior of members, timely attendance at worship, and care of the community. The informational queries related to administrative detail such as membership changes, births and deaths, and who had been recorded as ministers. Local meetings were required to send their responses to the yearly meeting annually.

By the early 1900s, the use of queries had changed enough that they were not used as much to establish a consistent manner of behavior among meetings. Newer queries became more devotional and seemed to encourage personal and corporate responses to issues of concern. Some yearly meetings still required local meetings to send along answers each year. Some queries came directly out of the collected advices that can be found in almost all historical books of discipline.

One important aspect of queries is in the expectation that each time an individual or a meeting looks deeply at a given query, the answer that comes forth might be different. Queries can help us rediscover old truths, look at things freshly, and support us in not becoming trapped in rigid practices without fresh light. A group may use a query for both comfort and discomfort, as part of the invitation to experience truths more deeply, fully, soulfully, experientially, and actively.

Northern Yearly Meeting Friends find the use of queries supportive of our personal and community efforts to learn about a concern and to respond to it. Regular use of queries is one portion of the discipline of our faith practices. They help us seek more deeply. They help us learn to listen and to receive glimmers of right knowledge. They help us reach discernment.

This edition of the Faith and Practice of Northern Yearly Meeting includes queries in each chapter. Effort has been made to write these queries so that in most cases it is not possible to give a simple Yes or No answer. The goal has been to support more detailed responses, new each time.

We encourage you to add your own queries, as you use these chapters.

Spiritual Beliefs of Friends in Northern Yearly Meeting

We hope we shall never finish considering our fundamental beliefs...
—Yearly Meeting of Aotearoa/New Zealand, 1991. (1)

Friends find their essential unity in their profound and exhilarating belief in the pervasive presence of God and in the continuing responsibility of each person and worshipping group to seek the leading of the Spirit in all things. Obedience to the leading of that Spirit rather than to any written statement of belief or conduct is the obligation of their faith.
—Faith and Practice of New England Yearly Meeting, 1985. (2)

While professing no creeds, we have strongly held beliefs for which Friends both past and present have suffered, gone to jail, and even died. While acknowledging the diversity of expression among Northern Yearly Meeting Friends we affirm the following common basis of faith.

We believe that within each person there is the Divine Spirit. We refer to this "true light that enlightens every one coming into the world" (John 1:9 WEB) by different names: the Light Within, the Inward Christ; that of God, the Seed, the Inward Teacher,

Holy Spirit, the Divine Companion, the Word, a Higher Power, and other names. In the 1700s, John Woolman stated this fundamental belief:

> *There is a principle which is pure, placed in the human mind, which in different places and ages hath had different names. It is, however, pure and proceeds from God. It is deep and inward, confined to no forms of religion nor excluded from any, where the heart stands in perfect sincerity.* (3)

Quakerism grew within Christianity and many of the terms reflect that. However, throughout our history, Quakers in giving testimony to their experience used a variety of other rich and descriptive religious languages that many today find meaningful, freeing, and more inclusive.

The expectation or the possibility that one may have a direct experience of the Divine remains a central testimony of Friends today. The Light Within is available to us all, and we seek to be attentive to it and to align ourselves with God's direction. Divine leadings guide our worship, our corporate business, and our personal lives. Thus, Divine revelation continues. We state with George Fox that "the Lord God is at work in this thick night." (4)

An inherent danger in claiming a direct experience with the Divine is misinterpretation of that experience, or leading, resulting in inappropriate action. Testing leadings against Scripture, Friends testimonies, and the Friends community can minimize this danger.

Individual and collective worship is waiting upon and listening for the voice of God. This practice is central to discerning Divine leading. Our corporate worship can be unprogrammed, semi-programmed, or programmed. Whatever the form, we state with John Woolman that we worship "...to distinguish the language of the pure Spirit which inwardly moves upon the heart." (5)

Spiritual Beliefs of Friends in Northern Yearly Meeting

Some Friends believe in this inner power which may be called love; yet do not identify the source of this power and love as being from an external Higher Power or God. These Friends share the belief that each person has worth and is precious and agree that everyone should be treated with dignity, mutual respect, and love.

We believe that all life is sacred; all people, as children of God, can be baptized by the Holy Spirit; that every meal has the potential to become a sacred means of receiving God's grace. We choose to emphasize the spiritual meaning of practices such as baptism and communion rather than the use of the outward forms. We understand communion to be those times when we truly experience the Divine Presence. We believe communion can be experienced at any time, alone or with others, at times other than worship.

Early Friends knew the Bible well and quoted it often. The Jewish and Christian writings of the Bible are still a rich source of inspiration, but not the only source of divine inspiration. Robert Barclay described this understanding of scripture in 1678:

> *The Scriptures...are not to be considered the principal foundation of all truth and knowledge. ...We truly know them only by the inward testimony of the Spirit...the Spirit is the primary and principal rule of faith.* (6)

Modern biblical scholarship and being open to the Spirit can help us understand the scriptures in new ways. Many Friends find inspiration in the sacred writings and meditative practices of other faith traditions and secular writings.

Friends believe we must lead our lives in congruence with our faith. Our inward experience of the living God comes through personal and collective worship, prayer, the scriptures, other devotional readings, and by other means. This brings spiritual growth, which in turn leads to the expression of divine leadings in our lives. We seek the wholeness that results from spirit-filled lives. These divine leadings have throughout our history led Quakers to repeated and consistent actions, which have come to be known as testimonies. Some of these testimonies are equality, peace, community, simplicity, and integrity.

Early Friends lived transformed lives that shook the unjust social and economic structure of their day. In like manner, let modern Friends seek to heed the voice of God to meet the immense challenges of our day.

Queries

For individuals:

1. How do I apply spiritual discernment in my life?
2. As I seek the Divine will, how am I open to finding it?
3. How do I rely on the Divine for the strength to follow leadings?
4. How do I make space in my life for reflection and meditation?

For meetings:

1. How does the meeting help lead members, attenders, and our children to an understanding of Friends' beliefs?
2. How do the testimonies shape the life of our meeting?
3. How does our meeting respond to differences in beliefs?

References:

1. Yearly Meeting of Aotearoa/New Zealand, *Questions and Counsel*, 1991, p. 2.
2. John Woolman, *The Journal and Major Essays of John Woolman*, ed. Phillips P. Moulton (Richmond, IN: Friends United Press, 1971), p. 236.
3. George Fox. Epistle 227 (written in 1663). http://esr.earlham.edu/qbi/gfe/e227-232.htm#e227 (accessed 5 September 2016).
4. Woolman, p. 31.
5. Robert Barclay, "Inspiration" (Proposition 3, The

Spiritual Beliefs of Friends in Northern Yearly Meeting

Scriptures), *Barclay's Apology in Modern English*, ed. Dean Freiday (Newberg , OR: Barclay Press 1991), p. 46.

Approved 2005

Testimonies –
A Bridge between Faith and Practice

...the testimonies grow out of our inward religious experience and are intended to give outward expression to the leading of the Spirit of God within;...

From the beginning Friends believed that they could have direct and immediate communication with God...[and] soon experienced certain common leadings of the Spirit.

They believed they must be convinced of the "truth" of the testimony each time they were called upon to enact it in their lives. Otherwise the testimonies would become lifeless rules of conduct...

—Wilmer Cooper, *The Testimony of Integrity in the Religious Society of Friends* (Pendle Hill Pamphlet #296, 1991), p. 7.

Care for the Earth

God saw all that he had made, and indeed, it was very good!
—Genesis 1:31. International Standard Version (ISV)

It would go a great way to caution and direct People in the Use of the World, that they were better studied and known in the Creation of it. For how can [people] find the Confidence to abuse it, while they should see the Great Creator stare them in the Face, in all and every Part thereof?
—William Penn, 1693. (1)

That as the mind was moved on an inward principle to love God as an invisible, incomprehensible being, on the same principle it was moved to love him in all his manifestations in the visible world; that as by his breath the flame of life was kindled in all animal and sensitive creatures, to say we love God as unseen and at the same time exercise cruelty toward the least creature moving by his life or by life derived from him was a contradiction in itself.
—John Woolman, ca. 1738. (2)

God calls Friends today...to look into our hearts and examine our relationship with the rest of Creation, and to

> *recognize that our neighbor includes the entire Earth community. We, too, are being asked to give up habits and things which have made our lives seem easier, just as slaves appeared to make life easier for their owners.*
> —Lisa Gould, 1994. (3)

Faith

Friends in Northern Yearly Meeting find spiritual nourishment in our connections to the natural world. As we care for pets or houseplants; walk to work; tend gardens or farms; hike or forage in the woods; or retreat to wild places for healing, we find a sense of reverence, renewal, connection to God, and unity with all Creation.

As individuals we have a wide variety of beliefs about God and many ways of describing and explaining our experience of God's presence in the natural world. Some Friends might say, "Humans are a part of nature, just like a fish or an elm tree. We're not special or separate" or "Christ is Lord of Creation. We humans are stewards—caretakers with the ability to see the whole web of nature and a responsibility to care for all of the earth with love and compassion." Others would say, "Gaia is a whole living being, and we are all a part of her." "Seeing God as inherent in all of creation, then we should not speak of a connection between Spirit and nature—they are one."

Many of us carry—sometimes with a sense of frustration and sometimes with joy and wonder at the paradox—both the image of humans as part of a whole Earth and that of humans as somehow estranged and alienated from that whole. However we try to explain it, we share a sense that our relationship to the Divine is intertwined with our relationship to the rest of Creation. Brokenness in our interactions with the natural world grows out of—and can feed—a sense of separation from Spirit.

Care for the Earth

Jesus said "...if you are offering your gift at the altar and there remember that your brother or sister has something against you, leave your gift there in front of the altar. First go and be reconciled to them; then come and offer your gift to God." (Matthew 5:23-24. NIV)

This reminds us that our relationship to God will only be whole or complete when we have been reconciled to those we have wronged or wounded. If the concept of "neighbor" is to be extended to include even our enemies, should we not also include the damaged creatures and natural systems of Earth among those brothers and sisters with whom we seek reconciliation?

History of This Concern

Since early history human beings around the world have been aware of and honored the sacred within nature because they knew their survival depended on the health of their immediate environment. The authors of Genesis, when reflecting on the creation, say repeatedly the refrain: "it was very good."

The writers of the Psalms knew that natural images can bring us into a sense of connection with the Divine, and in speaking of God often used natural images such as light, rock, water, and wind. Jesus too used images from nature when talking about humans' relationship to God. He spoke of good soil, sprouting seeds, and a fruitful vine. Other passages described a living spring of water, wind and fire, rock and sand, sowing and reaping. He also sought out the wilderness for times of personal renewal and connection with the Divine.

Early Friends, although focusing primarily on right relationships in the human community, were aware of the need to respect and care for the earth.

> *What wages doth the Lord desire of you for his earth that He giveth to you...but that you give him the praise*

and honour, and the thanks, and the glory; and not that you should spend the creatures upon your lusts, but to do good with them;...leave all creatures behind you as you found them, which God hath given to serve all nations and generations...
—George Fox, 1678. (4)

Friends' testimonies on simplicity, community, integrity, equality, and peace all remind us to use the gifts of creation wisely, not to take more than we need, and to be aware of the ways our actions affect others. More recently Friends have felt a need to speak more specifically about our responsibilities for stewardship and earth care. Northern Yearly Meeting first voiced these concerns as a body in 1988, approving this minute:

Gathering on Holy Ground, we are feeling a concern for nature, for God as well as what harm we are doing to God's creation. We perceive this as a spiritual concern. (5)

In 1993, another Northern Yearly Meeting minute stated,

We as Friends affirm our spiritual relationship with nature. Our concern for the earth is interwoven in all aspects of our lives, and we recognize that we are responsible for helping to maintain the precarious balance in all of Creation. (6)

Friends Committee on National Legislation's 1987 policy statement also spoke of this concern

The earth we share is limited in its capacity to support life and to provide resources for our survival. The environment that has provided sustenance for generations must be protected for generations to come. We have an

Care for the Earth

obligation, therefore, to be responsible stewards of the earth...(7)

Connections to Peace and Justice

Our growth-dependent economy, together with the brokenness in our interaction with the natural world, has ravaged and plundered the earth. Furthermore, four-fifths of all global fossil fuels and natural resources are controlled and consumed by 20% of the world's population. The exponential population growth of the world further adds to the growing inequality and suffering. The results of this plundering and inequality are a continuing pattern of wars and violations of human rights—people being deprived of freedom, basic human necessities, the opportunity to grow their own food, and of cultural and spiritual connections to their land and their communities.

> *For our own well-being, we need to respect God's creation or risk losing the loving sustenance God intends it to provide...When we carelessly treat our biosphere with lack of respect, we defy God, its creator. Such offenses harm not only the plants, animals, environment, and other people, but also...we are hurting ourselves.*
> —Diane J. Peterson, 1995. (8)

In 1763 in *A Plea for the Poor*, John Woolman urged Friends to examine their lives to see if there might be the "seeds of war" nourished "in these our possessions." (9) Today we seek to look closely not only at our homes, furniture, and garments but also at the food we eat, the transportation we choose, the ways we use our time and money, and our attitudes toward the earth. Are we sowing the seeds of renewal and healing—or of continued ecological decline and attendant resource wars?

FAITH AND PRACTICE

Practice

Friends endeavor to live joyfully, mindfully, and with reverent regard for the natural world, supporting one another and keeping this leading [care for the earth and its natural systems] a discernible element of living in the manner of Friends.
—Alden McCutchan, 2001. (10)

How do Northern Yearly Meeting Friends live this testimony? Some individual Friends have carried this question as a spiritual concern and have worked both to reduce their own eco-footprints and to encourage their meetings to pay greater attention to environmental issues. Many Friends have made changes in household routines, such as composting, recycling, and conservation. Some Friends have made larger lifestyle changes, such as limiting the size of their families and eliminating use of their cars and air travel.

In recent years many meetings have included energy conservation practices in the design and care of their meetinghouses. Some meetings have joined with other churches or community groups to reach out to the public concerning environmental issues.

Friends are increasingly alarmed about global warming/climate change. After many years during which environmental concerns were carried primarily by individuals, we now see the beginnings of corporate concern and witness.

Some Friends have smaller ecological footprints than others. No matter how careful we are, we know we use more resources than most people on the planet. In the *State of the Society with Attention to Earthcare,* approved by Northern Yearly Meeting in June, 2001, Friends acknowledged:

...at times we participate in activities we know to be harmful to the Earth and to ourselves. Simply by living

where we do, in the culture of the United States, we each contribute daily to the global eco-crisis. Knowing this, many of us struggle with feelings of frustration or despair, wishing we could change, but not seeing a way forward. Economic survival, comfort, community connections, and convenience for ourselves and our families are often major factors in our decisions. (11)

We feel an urgency to change the way we live. We struggle with the complexity and difficulty of the necessary changes, and with our feelings of guilt and powerlessness. We grieve deeply the entangling complicity of our involvement. Each of us comes to this concern from his/her own point on the path and needs to discern the right next step. We need to uphold each other with compassion and help each other as we seek to open ourselves to the leadings of the Spirit. We will differ in the details of our leadings, but every step toward healing in our relationship to the natural world will also bring healing and growth in our spiritual lives. As this growth opens us to the Divine, we trust that we will all see and hear more clearly where we are next called to act.

We struggle. We celebrate. We live our lives as best we can. We wait and live in the Light. We search for individual and corporate discernment. We pray for Divine guidance and for the strength to follow it. (12)

Queries

For individuals:

1. What hinders my ability to be in harmony with earth's systems? What parts of my life are in conflict with the integrity of these systems?
2. What are the barriers I struggle with as I move toward unity with nature? As I use resources and energy, do I encounter

my shadow (being mindful of both shadow and Light within)? What do our deep shadows teach us?
3. How do I express gratitude for all that has been freely given? How do I find support to face emotional and intellectual conflicts and move toward healing?
4. As life-changing events (e.g. becoming a family, retiring, moving) cycle into life, how do we support one another in clarifying and making changes that will be more environmentally sustaining?
5. What burden does our waste place on future generations?

For individuals or groups:

1. How do we respond to the statement: There is that of God not only in every human person, but in every element of Creation?"
2. When did I/we last experience a sense of wonder?
3. How will we cultivate and deepen a sense of wonder to live in the virtue of a more reverent life?
4. How will we weave self, nature, and the Divine into spiritual unity?
5. How do we use awareness of beauty and imaginative abilities to be in a place where transformation can occur?

For meetings:

1. How do we share the depth of our gratitude, pleasure, and joy in the natural world with our children? How do we share our concerns and our discernment with our children?
2. What is our vision of how Friends could work together to be "patterns and examples" of a spirit-centered and truly sustainable way of life? What steps could we take toward making this vision a living witness?
3. How can we encourage careful consideration of our relationship to the earth among our members and partner with movements offering a positive vision of a way forward?

4. How do we treat prophetic voices in our meeting? How does the meeting respond to an acknowledged concern?

References:

1. William Penn, "Reflections and Maxims, #12 and #13," *Some Fruits of Solitude*. The Harvard Classics (New York: P. F. Collier & Son, 1909–14).
2. John Woolman, Journal in *The Journal and Major Essays of John Woolman*, ed. Phillips Moulton, Richmond, Indiana, Friends United Press, 1971, p. 28.
3. Lisa Gould, *Friends, Slavery, and the Earth*, Quaker Earthcare Witness pamphlet, 1994. http://www.quakerearthcare.org/article/friends-slavery-and-earth (Accessed 23 July 2016).
4. George Fox, *The Works of George Fox*, vol. IV, *Gospel Truth Demonstrated in a Collection of Doctrinal Books Given Forth by That Faithful Minister of Jesus Christ, George Fox* (Philadelphia, Marcus T. C. Gould; New York, Isaac T. Hopper, 1831), p. 321. https://archive.org/stream/works-georgefox06foxgoog#page/n328/mode/1up (Accessed 23 July 2016)
5. Northern Yearly Meeting. *The Minutes of Northern Yearly Meeting of the Religious Society of Friends*. 1988.
6. Northern Yearly Meeting. *The Minutes of Northern Yearly Meeting of the Religious Society of Friends*. 1993.
7. Friends Committee on National Legislation, Legislative Policy Statement, 1987; quoted in: "Spiritual Reflections on Unity with Nature," Baltimore Yearly Meeting Ad Hoc Committee on Unity With Nature. http://www.un-documents.net/values/srouwn.htm (Accessed 23 July 2016)
8. Diane J. Peterson, Twin Cities Friends Meeting. 1995.
9. John Woolman, "A Plea for the Poor" in: *The Journal and Major Essays of John Woolman*, p. 255.

10. Alden McCutchan, "Proposed Earthcare Leading," *The Minutes of Northern Yearly Meeting of the Religious Society of Friends*, Northern Yearly Meeting, June 2001.
11. Northern Yearly Meeting. "State of Society with Attention to Earthcare," *The Minutes of Northern Yearly Meeting of the Religious Society of Friends*, 2001, p. 73.
12. Northern Yearly Meeting. *The Minutes of Northern Yearly Meeting of the Religious Society of Friends*, p. 73.

Approved 2009

Integrity

While seeking to interpret our Christian faith in the language of today, we must remember that there is one worse thing than failure to practice what we profess, and that is to water down our profession to match our practice.
—Friends World Conference, 1952. (1)

When you live with integrity, that implies a spiritually integrated wholeness where you live in the world but remain spiritually beyond it. Since your actions express who you are, a person with integrity reflects a considered response to life, attuned to the leadings of that of God within.
—Patty Weerts, 1999. (2)

The concept of completeness/wholeness is the most powerful thought for me. If each aspect of ourselves is developed and is brought together into a unified spirit, we will be made whole, and how much more difficult it will be to fall out of step with the Spirit when all aspects of our being are working in concert together.
—Sheila Thomas, 1999. (3)

Integrity is a wholeness that comes when actions are in accordance with beliefs. When we act with integrity, we do so, not out of a willful self-denial but out of an honest understanding of our beliefs. This requires that we be clear about our beliefs, both with ourselves and with others.

To be clear in our beliefs in a way that will make integrity possible in our lives, we strive to understand what is truth, what is merely factually accurate, and what is false. Truths that we are to act upon exist above and beyond our limited ability to grasp them fully. Therefore, we need not only the gifts we are given but also reference points beyond ourselves to guide us in our discernment of truth. One process is to engage in a spiritual dialogue with the Inner Guide. Reference points include others in our current and historical spiritual community with whom we can test our insights.

Integrity enables one to live in the world while remaining spiritually centered. Acting with integrity demands that we accept responsibility for our actions and our reactions to the world.

All aspects of one's self are affected. One's needs, values, words, and actions are congruent. Integrity leads us to truthfulness, fairness, and a resolve to do that which is right.

Each decision that we make influences future choices and possible options. Because we cannot fully predict the outcome of our actions, we strive to engage in right action and not focus on outcomes alone. Right and just means are all that we can provide. There is faith that if we engage in right actions, the fruits of those actions will be right. The outcome is left in the hands of the Spirit by which our lives are guided.

We strive to be open to re-examining our beliefs and understandings so that we can grow. This is done through an openness to the Spirit and a willingness to change as truth is revealed. We must act out of our beliefs at each given moment in time, but as we are led by the Spirit into new understanding, we are willing to act in accord with the greater knowledge. Therefore, integrity does not imply that we will act the same in any given situation

Integrity

each time it is faced. Rather, integrity demands that we act to our highest level of understanding in all situations, as they occur.

Integrity requires the ability to be steadfast in times of ease and in times of difficulty or even danger. It can be harder to maintain integrity in difficult times when there is a temptation to take the easy route or when societal pressures are inconsistent with our beliefs.

We strive to follow through on commitments, take responsibility for our actions, and remain true to our beliefs. We also strive to grow personally, acting not primarily out of self-interest but in the interest in doing what is right according to our faith.

Integrity is essential, but it is not sufficient. Other values are incomplete without integrity, and integrity without the temperance of other spiritually centered values can degenerate into rigidity. Tempering our sense of what is right with compassion, understanding, and tolerance of other people's experience of truth will help prevent us from acting out of our own beliefs in ways that may harm others.

There is both personal integrity and group integrity. As a group, Friends have the responsibility to maintain the long-standing reputation in the wider community of fairness and honest dealings. We also strive to deal with each other in our own spiritual community with a loving honesty and sensitivity to the leadings of others. Each member of a community contributes to its overall level of integrity and its ability to weave together diverse elements to create a cohesive, integrated whole.

Queries

For individuals:

1. In which ways do I regularly examine the way my life speaks in relation to my beliefs?

2. How do I maintain or regain an inner unity when there is a conflict between my faith and my practice?
3. How do I behave with integrity within the meeting and the wider community?
4. How does my faith and integrity inform my work?

For meetings:

1. How does our meeting nurture the integrity of each individual?
2. How does our meeting nurture the integrity of the meeting and its committees?
3. In what ways does our meeting manifest its integrity in the wider community?
4. How does our meeting sustain and strengthen the integrity of Quakerism?
5. How do meetings open themselves to receive words lovingly from a Friend who speaks from a place of integrity, even when that Friend challenges, confronts, or ministers to the meeting in a way that makes it uneasy?

References:

1. Friends World Conference "Third World conference of Friends: held at Oxford, England 28th July – 6th August, 1952." London: 1952, p. xvi.
2. Patty Weerts, Fox Valley Friends Meeting Fall Gathering Workshop on Integrity, 1999.
3. Sheila Thomas, Fox Valley Friends Meeting Fall Gathering Workshop on Integrity, 1999.

Approved 2005

Peace

The Quaker witness for peace is as relevant today as ever and speaks powerfully to a world afflicted with suffering, violence, and war. We have a vision of a peaceable kingdom, here and now, in which the Divine leads us to reject violence in any form.

The peace testimony of early Friends was rooted in their personal experience of the love and power of Christ. When George Fox was offered release from prison if he would serve in Cromwell's army he responded:

> *I told [the Commonwealth Commissioners] I lived in the virtue of that life and power that took away the occasion for all wars....I told them that I was come into the covenant of peace which was before wars and strife were.*
> —George Fox, 1651. (1)

> *Wars arise from inner desires—that is where the conflict begins. Because God resolved that conflict in the heart of George Fox through the victory of the Lamb, George Fox could not participate in outward wars. War was obsolete; his life was centred in love.*
> —Michael Birkel, 2004. (2)

This peace testimony of the early Quakers was not based on some principle that they developed, but on their experience of Divine grace through which they came into the covenant of peace.

The peaceable kingdom is the kingdom of God. On a fundamental level this means that we enter the kingdom through God's love (grace) and not through our own struggling. The kingdom of peace is a gift. We do not build it with our hands, although we are called to be faithful citizens of this kingdom with all of our hearts, minds, and strength.
—Sandra Cronk, 1984. (3)

Do not conform to the pattern of this world, but be transformed by the renewing of your mind. Then you will be able to test and approve what God's will is—his good pleasing and perfect will.
—Romans 12:2 (NIV)

The peace testimony is our witness to the world of a transformed life centered in love. To have an experiential knowledge of the Divine changes our hearts, our relationships, and our desires. We aspire to be rooted in this transforming power. We hope to experience this power that makes us incapable of acts of violence and oppression and gives us "the peace that passes all understanding." We try to manifest this inner peace in the often-troubled world that surrounds us. This peace witness begins in our own hearts and lives. Jesus' great commandment was to love. That love can ripple out in ever widening circles, starting with ourselves, our families, our faith communities, then to our nation and the entire world, including our enemies. This love requires compassion but living our lives centered in this love also requires constructive action that seeks an end to poverty, violence, and suffering.

God's grace can transform our lives; it releases us from hatred and offers an invitation to others to be transformed. We envision an end to war but the peace testimony calls us to more than that; it calls us to a peaceable kingdom here on earth now. The Kingdom of God is within us; we bring a message of good news as an alternative to war and violence.

Violence is real and pervasive in our world. We support the role of the state in constraining people from hurting others, and we recognize that organized violence requires organized constraint. What we do not support is the use of violence, injustice, and discrimination as a means to this end. We are grateful to those who keep us safe, and we honor them with our respect and compassion, even as we seek to spread nonviolence among them. We utterly oppose killing, capital punishment, and violent tactics of any kind. We seek to minister with respect and compassion to victims and perpetrators alike and to all those who work with them. We seek to be present with all parties to conflict.

Individual Quakers and Quaker meetings have struggled to discern their leading with respect to witnessing to the peaceable kingdom. There is great diversity among us regarding the question of whether some violence can reach a point where it can no longer be constrained by nonviolent means. Some Friends have been led to be conscientious participants in the effort to constrain violence, even to the point of participating in physical forms of constraint.

As Quakers seeking to live in the life and power that takes away all occasion for war, the following principles witness to our testimony:

We Repudiate War

We seek a world that chooses nonviolent means to accomplish its goals and seeks to heal the hates and hurts of individuals and nations. We hold that it is inconsistent with our religious testimony to participate in violent struggle and therefore we support those who take the stand as conscientious objectors to war and violence. We ask, "Can war truly be the will of God?" We recognize the bravery and commitment of those who fight on every side, and we extend compassion to all who suffer for any reason.

We Seek To Stop Preparation for War

We work for disarmament. We seek to transform all war-devoted technology, industry, commerce and political activity into peace-devoted alternatives.

> *...they shall beat their swords into plowshares...*
> —Micah 4:3 (NRSV)

We support those who resist the war system with civil disobedience such as refusing to pay war-related taxes; choosing to live simply, below the taxable level; refusing to register for the draft; or blockading war preparation activities. And we support those who return from war to civilian life.

We Seek To Eliminate the Seeds of War

We work for social and economic justice and for the right sharing of world resources. We seek an Earth restored by a deep reverence for the natural processes that sustain all life, so that all people may breathe and drink and harvest without fear. We seek to move toward a vision of our population in balance with the rest of creation, so that undue pressure on scarce resources is not the root of conflict. We strive to share and celebrate our differences and to live in harmony with all our inevitable conflicts.

We Seek To Sow the Seeds of Peace

These principles are focused on the important and essential work of prevention to which many of us are called in diverse ways. But the real heart of the peace testimony is not prevention but transformation—being transformed by God's love. This is a radical vision of the peaceable kingdom; a vision that through faithful lives our energy can shift from fear and prevention to love and nurture.

We are all connected. A more peaceful and compassionate world is as close as reaching out to strangers and friends alike and letting peace radiate from each of our lives. This is work to which all of us are called daily—we need only listen and respond. Our job is to live into the Light in the different ways that we are led, and trust that our work together will lead us toward a safer and more peaceful world.

> *He has told you...what does the Lord require of you but to do justice, and to love kindness, and to walk humbly with your God?*
> —Micah 6:8 (NRSV)

Queries

For individuals:

1. How do I nurture peacefulness in my own heart?
2. How does my life reflect the need for peace in my family, meeting, community and the workplace
3. What do I do about domestic violence, prison violence, police violence and violence in entertainment?
4. What daily activities support peace building?
5. What do I do about institutional violence?
6. How can I cease supporting war?

For meetings:

1. What does the meeting do to bring our peace witness to the wider community and the world?
2. How does the meeting live out the peace testimony within its own practice?

3. How does the meeting teach and practice the peace testimony with your youth?
4. How is our peace testimony grounded in right relationship with all creation?
5. How does the meeting learn ways of peace from other groups and communities?

References:

1. George Fox, *The Journal of George Fox,* ed. John L. Nickalls, 1651, as quoted in Britain Yearly Meeting *Quaker Faith & Practice*, Third Edition, 1995. 24.01.
2. Michael Birkel, *Silence and Witness* (Maryknoll, NY: Orbis Books, 2004), p. 115.
3. Sandra Cronk, *Peace Be With You, A Study of the Spiritual Basis of the Friends Peace Testimony*. Tract of the Association of Friends. 1984. p. 11. http://www.tractassociation.org/pamphlets/peace-you-study-spiritual-basis-friends-peace-testimony/ (accessed 23 July 2016).

Approved 2008

Equality

There is neither Jew nor Greek, there is neither slave nor free, there is no male and female, for you are all one in Christ Jesus.
—Galatians 3:28 (ESV)

Do rightly, justly, truly, holy, equally to all people in all things; and that is according to that of God in every [person] and the witness of God.
—George Fox, 1661. (1)

Love is the hardest lesson in Christianity; but for that reason, it should be most our care to learn it.
—William Penn, 1693.(2)

The excitement of the very first Friends was the radical understanding that the Divine is still present in all of creation. God is present in all things and speaks afresh in new and different languages to each. The transcendence of God humbles us, invites us to wait in Meeting for Worship. The understanding that any of the individuals gathered in community for worship may be the one to share Light underpins all of our desire to fully practice the testimony of equality. This understanding gives foundation for each next step beyond the time of deep worship.

Early Quakers became buoyed up by these mystical discoveries. They found great freedom from the rigid requirements of class, church hierarchies, and wealth. They shared their leadings and practiced this freedom in very public ways. Women, men, and children shared the opportunities and responsibilities for worship, ministry, and care of their community. These Quakers carried their faith far out into their world and tried to live it daily amid the turbulence of their time.

A century later, the *Journal* of John Woolman conveyed his lifelong compassion, curiosity, and desire to know more fully and understand the spirit of each individual and community he encountered. He yearned to share some of the Divine Truth he himself had experienced.

> *Having for many years felt love in my heart toward the natives of this land who dwell far back in the wilderness...I felt inward drawings towards a visit to that place.*
>
> *Love was the first motion,...that I might feel and understand their life and the spirit they live in, if haply I might receive some instruction from them, or they be in any degree helped forward by my following the leadings of Truth among them.*
> —John Woolman (3)

Friends still carry Woolman's vision of the fullness of life for everyone. This belief in the potential for Divine Light coming from many directions does not give us all knowledge. It cautions us to dwell deeply, to listen mindfully, to walk with humility, and to lovingly hold each other accountable for the ways we walk with one another. We earnestly desire that the world will see us as people who do good things. We too easily make judgments that the ways we choose to live must be the ways all others should walk. Again and again, we are humbled by our desire to nurture, but our inability to see the next right step.

We trust that by opening ourselves to listen for the Divine in

Equality

us, and sharing that in verbal and active witness, we affirm our equality. Every time we gather with others, whether for worship or other activities, the opportunity opens for new understanding of the fullness of this testimony. Northern Yearly Meeting has welcomed numerous exchanges with the evangelical El Salvador Yearly Meeting (Junta Annual de la Iglesia Evangelica de los Amigos en El Salvador). There is an on-going conversation which challenges both yearly meetings to listen for the spirit within the words and for those unspoken words discerned during worship. Our Friend, Raul Perez, from El Salvador Yearly Meeting, described his joy after meeting with us:

> ...when there is a spirit that moves us our differences can be seen as a gift from God that makes us rich and not as an inconvenience that can cause discomfort. (4)

Mere professing is never sufficient. Northern Yearly Meeting is reaching in and out to experience more fully the deepest meanings of being inclusive and nurturing. We want to recognize and celebrate diversity. We are called to act wherever we see inequality. We want to engage with each other and our wider communities now to create opportunities for this vision of a more just society. Justice can only be served when all those involved can understand the consequences and engage with one another to bring positive results into being.

Sometimes we fail to live up to our Light. We need to seek forgiveness from and reconciliation with those we seem to have shut out and simply have not noticed. We need to extend compassion and forgiveness to those who wound us. Both giving and receiving respect and support can be wrapped in the Divine Love that gathers us together as Friends.

We ask the support of one another as we actively work to help this testimony transform our practice, so that we do truly meet the Divine in every neighbor.

Everything...is grounded in the truth that there is that of God within each of us...we each can know love, truth, and therefore wholeness, fully."
—Niyonu D. Spann, 2007 (5)

Queries

For individuals:

1. What will I do to live my beliefs about equality?
2. Where do I see inequality in the world and how do I address it?
3. How can I become more aware of my own biases? Am I humble in receiving others' perceptions?
4. How can I respond to differences with interest and respect?
5. How can I overcome my fear of difference? Fear of getting it wrong?

For meetings:

1. How can we see each other as equals? Or how can we see the divine in each person?
2. How do we address inequality in the world?
3. What practices do we use to acknowledge and nurture that of God in every one?
4. How do we celebrate diversity? How do we value our differences?
5. What is our spirit-given Truth, the truth which makes us both vulnerable and bold?

References:

1. George Fox, 1661, "Epistle 200." A collection of many select and Christian epistles, letters and testimonies, written on sundry occasions, by that ancient, eminent, faithful Friend and minister of Christ Jesus, George Fox. Pg. 192. http://esr.earlham.edu/qbi/gfe/e200-206.htm.

Equality

2. William Penn, 1693. Britain Yearly Meeting, *Quaker Faith & Practice*, 22.01, 1995.
3. John Woolman, *Journal* in *The Journal and Major Essays of John Woolman,* ed. Phillips Moulton, Richmond, IN, Friends United Press, 1971, pp. 122–3, 127.
4. Raul Perez, letter, *Northern Yearly Meeting Newsletter*, 8,2011, p. 14.
5. Niyonu D. Spann, "Beyond Diversity 101: Toward living, true community," in Friends General Conference *FG Connections,* Autumn 2007.

Approved 2015

Simplicity

Life is meant to be lived from a Center, a divine Center....a life of unhurried peace and power. It is simple. It is serene. It is amazing. It takes no time, but it occupies all our time.
—Thomas Kelly, 1941. (1)

Simplicity does not mean drabness or narrowness but is essentially positive, being the capacity for selectivity in one who holds attention on the goal. Thus simplicity is an appreciation of all that is helpful toward living as children of the Living God.
—North Carolina Yearly Meeting (Conservative), 1983. (2)

Simplicity is essential to our relationship with the Divine. It is the deepest leading of spiritual life in stewarding needs, time, money, possessions, and energy for the purpose of our relationship with the Divine. Inward and visible simplicity are the characteristic way, sign, and witness to the spiritual life of Friends.

Simplicity can set free richness of spiritual life and joy in living. It nurtures creativity and sensitivity to the natural world and is a sturdy, functional, and serviceable guide to our lives. It can remove barriers to engagement with others. This testimony encourages Friends to consider obstacles in our lives, which interfere with this Divine experience.

Faith and Practice

Quakers affirm the needs of the physical life, beauty, artistic expression, and community life. Friends recognize that simplicity manifests itself in diverse ways within each life and among lives in the same community. The practice of this testimony changes throughout our lives and requires a constant awareness. We recognize the pressures to conform to the materialism of our society. Discernment, with the assistance of the wider Quaker community, supports intentional development of practical applications.

Friends' public witness to the testimony of simplicity promotes equity in the distribution of resources, sustainable economic development, and long-term care of the natural world. It is the result of Friends' seeking the Divine and discerning how they are led to live from this Center.

Frances Taber, a contemporary Friend writes:

> *It may surprise some of us to hear that the first generation of Friends did not have a testimony for simplicity. They came upon a faith which cut to the root of the way they saw life, radically reorienting it. They saw that all they did must flow directly from what they experienced as true, and that if it did not, both the knowing and the doing became false. In order to keep the knowledge clear and the doing true, they stripped away anything which seemed to get in the way. They called those things superfluities, and it is this radical process of stripping for clear-seeing which we now term simplicity.* (3)

Many nineteenth century Friends carried this radical process to excess. They exercised an outward practice in dress and lifestyle that, long after it has been abandoned, leaves a false impression that Quakers are most notable for their austerity and plainness.

Listen to Frances Taber again:

> *The taproot of simplicity is to be found at that point in*

Simplicity

the life of a Friend when the realization comes that his or her inner and outer lives are connected, that for the inward life to continue to grow, there must be a response from the outward life. It is at that point where awareness dawns that spiritual knowledge itself comes from an open relationship between one's inner and outer lives, and from a free movement between the two. (4)

Queries

For individuals:

1. What does simplicity mean at this time in my life?
2. What am I attached to that distracts me from the Divine?
3. How do I integrate my inner life and my outward life?
4. The Gospel of Matthew asks, Where is your treasure? (Matthew 6:19-21)
5. How do I advocate for the application of simplicity in public life and policies?
6. When may external conspicuous display be appropriate?
7. How do I relate simplicity to our other testimonies?

For meetings:

1. How do we live out the Simplicity Testimony in our meeting?
2. How does our meeting support and encourage individuals to remove barriers to relationships with the Divine?
3. How does the testimony of simplicity affect celebrations, holiday programs, weddings and memorials?

References:

1. Thomas R. Kelly, *A Testament of Devotion* (New York: Harper and Brothers, 1941), pp. 116 and 124.
2. North Carolina Yearly Meeting, Conservative, *Faith and Practice,* 1983 Revision, p. 7.

3. Frances Irene Taber, "Finding the Taproot of Simplicity: The Movement between Inner Knowledge and Outer Action," in Leonard Stout Kenworthy, ed., *Friends Face the World: Some Continuing and Current Quaker Concerns.* Published cooperatively by Friends General Conference (Philadelphia, PA) and Friends United Press (Richmond, IN), 1987, p. 59. These quotes are also available on pages 5 and 6 of Pendle Hill Pamphlet #400, (2009) by Irene Tabor with the same title as the book chapter.
4. Taber, p. 59

Approved 2006

Community

And let us consider how we may spur one another on toward love and good deed, not giving up meeting together, as some are in the habit of doing, but let us encourage one another...
—Hebrews 10:24-25 (NIV)

To Friends, to know one another in the Light...meet together, and in the measure of God's spirit wait. That with it all, your minds may be guided up to God, to receive Wisdom from God. That you may all come to know how you may walk [in God's] wisdom...And Friends, meet together, and know one another in that which is eternal, which was before the world was...Therefore, in the Light, wait and walk, that you may have fellowship one with another.
—George Fox, 1657 (1)

Unless the meeting for worship is the center of the Quaker community...community is non-existent, the meeting is peripheral, and the Society of Friends just an organization with a membership list.
—Mildred Binns Young, 1959 (2)

Friends are called to live as a gathered people of God. As Friends meet together, we come to know one another in a spiritual dimension as well as the social dimension. In our Quaker meeting community we seek to discover together the truth of who we are. In community we celebrate and grieve life's transitions. We are nurtured and challenged. We enjoy fellowship and engage in service as we care for each other and the wider community. Together, we invite awareness of the presence of the Spirit in our worship and work. Together, we listen for the Spirit's leadings.

A longing for spiritual connection brings us into community. Our disciplined steady practice of being present with one another reflects and feeds this hunger. As we become one in the Spirit, each brings different gifts and concerns. The deepening community draws on these gifts and supports our emotional needs to know one another and to be known. This fellowship increases the challenges and work needed to respond to the various tasks within the community and beyond it.

To nurture this community we learn to temper our individual understandings so we may unite with others in a larger experience. This is not a sacrifice by individuals for the common good but a gift from God to all, a testimony to our faith in the Spirit as revealed in community. In a community that recognizes that bits of the Truth are scattered through our differences, we have learned that we can grow through these differences. We test our individual understandings through our practices of discernment, such as clearness committees or spiritual nurture groups. These practices lay the foundation for embracing diversity and living in harmony with conflict. When we feel seen, heard and cared for, we can be listened into wholeness.

When listening for the Spirit unifies us corporately and when we share a common experience of Presence, we call that a "gathered meeting." This can happen in small committee meetings, in monthly meetings for business, in meeting for worship, or in any gathering or work that is open to movement of Spirit. When decision-making is involved we call this unity the sense of the meet-

Community

ing. Unity in the sense of the Meeting does not mean that we agree on every point but that we set aside individual understandings to unite in a larger experience. Our willingness to be guided by Spirit is revealed by meeting and listening carefully to the Divine Presence. This practice of openness and respectful listening can become the patterning principle of our lives, influencing our conduct in all our relationships and circumstances.

Nurturing the life of this beloved meeting requires spiritual hospitality. This includes the spiritual preparation of individuals to dare to deeply engage with each other, to trust, and to be vulnerable. It also requires a suitable gathering place so that all may enter. Hospitality is both the invitation to participate and the removal of barriers such as time or access.

Nourishing this community may begin with preparing and eating food together. Regular community meals support the fellowship and connection that helps build scattered lives into a community of trust and welcome. Friends support one another through births, deaths, marriages, divorces, unemployment, moving households, and illnesses. One of the most tangible ways a community assists families or individuals facing difficulties is to provide meals or company during mealtime.

Community connection means we encounter both the easy and the difficult aspects of life. Friends endeavor to nourish and support one another through all of life's joys and sorrows. Waiting and listening are spiritual practices that may be used when a member faces spiritual, emotional, material, or physical challenges. Support should include honest awareness of what the meeting can and cannot provide.

Intervisitation enriches the meetings for worship, shares yearly meeting resources, and deepens our friendships. Visiting carries the energy and spirit of our annual gatherings on into the year and helps to deepen our understanding of one another. The community of Northern Yearly Meeting is nurtured by traveling Friends who visit our scattered meetings.

Our community is a living body of many parts, which varies from meeting to meeting and from individual to individual. Spiritual and social concerns link us with neighbors and people elsewhere. For some, spiritual needs and sensitivities lead us to other groups in our seeking. In these widening ways, as we respect each other's leadings, our Friends community can be enriched and broadened. We find our own understanding deepened; we hope our neighbor's is also.

The fellowship that George Fox told us we would experience can become a haven of welcome each time we gather in meeting for worship. We find nurture and deep bubbling joy as we come to know one another and be known. Our worship is deepened anew by each community member who joins in, and together, we can experience that place beyond words.

> *Our life is love, and peace, and tenderness; and bearing one with another, and forgiving one another, and not laying accusations against another; but praying one for another, and helping one another up with a tender hand.*
> —Isaac Penington, 1667 (3)

Queries

For individuals:

1. How do I practice spiritual hospitality?
2. Where do I find love and joy in my meeting community?
3. How do I invite others to participate?
4. How have I removed barriers?
5. What gifts and life experiences can I bring?
6. How do I balance the needs of others with my own needs?
7. How does this change at various stages of our lives?

Community

8. How do I support others in their leadings?

For meetings:

1. How do we deepen our spiritual connections?
2. How do we identify and communicate our unspoken expectations within the meeting?
3. How do we resolve and heal divisive situations?
4. What happens to the meeting community when individuals bring a wide range of perspectives and beliefs?
5. How does our fellowship support our worship?
6. How are decisions regarding meeting location, comfort, accessibility, aesthetics, financial practices and meeting tasks fundamental to creating and supporting community?
7. How does our community offer alternatives to the world's materialism and excessive individualism?
8. How well does our meeting respond to the challenge and messiness of day-to-day life as a community?
9. How does the community support Friends who are separated from the meeting?
10. How does our meeting strengthen community with other meetings?
11. How do the meetings of Northern Yearly Meeting strengthen community with each other?

Approved 2014

Community Support for Discernment and Committees of Clearness

The meeting community offers Friends many opportunities to accompany one another through times of challenge including decisions about life path, relationships, work, leadings to ministry, changes in health, aging, and even facing death. We have no history of naming pastors, yet all meeting communities will experience the need for various forms of practical pastoral care and nurture for members from time to time.

When life presents difficult decisions for discernment, our desire to care for one another provides the opportunity for the meeting to offer support and nurture through committees for clearness. As meeting communities become places where we feel deeply seen and heard, we can lift up our vulnerabilities and our difficulties in the presence of one another. Attentive listening is fundamental to how we may assist one another to reach discernment and clearness in times of personal challenge and need.

When community members desire support in the process of making particular decisions or experience dilemmas that require spiritual care, they may request a clearness committee to assist their discernment of Spirit moving in their lives.

Discernment is our search to know the true movement of Spirit and how we are called to respond. It helps us separate the wheat from the chaff. This may mean sorting out and letting go of that which is no longer useful.

Clearness describes the result of our search; we become clear. We experience deep inner assurance.

Clearness committees are used in the process of applying for membership or seeking to be married under the care of the meeting, and suggestions about the role of clearness committees in preparation for marriage is addressed after that chapter (page

Community

104) of this Faith and Practice. A meeting may also engage a clearness committee for issues that seem difficult for the meeting to resolve. Community members may request a clearness committee to support or assist their discernment. The guidelines and queries offered here may assist a meeting in providing clearness committees for all of these possibilities.

Each monthly meeting or worship group establishes general patterns of creating clearness committees, when they are desired. There may be a standing committee that is responsible for receiving requests for clearness committees and overseeing their practices. A seasoned Friend might be appointed to convene the group. Others are invited to join who are committed to deep listening and allowing the person seeking discernment to find his or her own way to the next steps. It is helpful if not all the persons on the committee are well known to the person seeking assistance. At times, an individual may call together others from the meeting to support a need or decision. Each clearness committee serves only in response to a given issue, with a new committee formed in response to each request. The work of each committee should be held as deeply confidential.

Committee meetings are to be surrounded with worship, which gathers the committee into the ability to listen more fully. Members participate by providing queries related to the issue and by reflecting back what they believe they have heard. Members may share personal resources and gifts but should not give advice or bring their own solutions to the issue.

Members are reminded that one meeting may not be sufficient; and in fact, clearness in the form of a definite next step or a solution to a problem may not ultimately be reached. If the person has a need that continues for some time, a continuing or new group may be asked to convene over a longer period of time. This group can become a trusting and intimate support environment in which to explore ongoing resources in response to the need.

Longer-term needs may move the group away from being a clearness committee per se, toward the creation of a nurture, support, or care committee for persons experiencing long-term needs or difficult circumstances.

A clearness process is not a therapy group, and a list of resources in the community outside the meeting should be available for further support when members understand that the one seeking assistance needs help beyond what the meeting can offer.

The invitation to serve on a clearness committee is not to be taken lightly. Each request requires us to seek clarity about our energy and ability to serve at that particular time and with that particular concern.

Committee members are encouraged to remember that the Light being sought is not our own understanding but is the Light of the Divine Spirit. All who serve must be able to bring respect for all present, a willingness to listen deeply, and compassion for the vulnerability of the individual seeking support.

Queries for Clearness Committees

1. Do you practice the discipline of listening for the spiritual meaning of words the speaker prefers?
2. How do you hold to the discipline that whatever is offered during the committee meeting is confidential?
3. Do you trust that Spirit can guide the individual and the committee? Do you keep heart and mind open for new answers?
4. Is sufficient care given to delegate the clerking of the meeting and to identify a recorder if such is deemed to be helpful?
5. Does the committee focus on the concern as it is currently presented without drawing out long history or past issues?
6. If asked to serve, will you be able to devote the time needed to adequately serve with this committee?
7. How do we distinguish between inspiration and impulse as we seek discernment?

References:

1. George Fox, Epistle 149, as published in "The Power of the Lord Is Over All", *The Pastoral Letters of George Fox*, Introduced and Edited by T. Canby Jones (Richmond, IN: Friends United Press, 1989), p. 114.
2. Mildred Binns Young, *Another Will Gird You* (Pendle Hill Pamphlet #109, 1959), p. 18.
3. Issac Pennington,"To Friends in Amersham" (1667) and *Britain Yearly Meeting Faith & Practice*, 5th edition, 2013, 10.01.

Approved November 2015

FAITH AND PRACTICE

Blessed are the Quakers who are the mystics, the
    scientists, educators, the cooks, the window washers,
    the holders, the healers, the privileged,
        for together we can build.

Blessed are the truth sayers, the contrary ones, the poets,
    the seekers, the doubters, the believers,
        for together they can shake the foundations.

Blessed are those in community,
        because they are not alone.

Blessed are those who reach under the fence, over the
    wall, across the divide,
        for they will show us the way.

Blessed are the risk takers, who step out of comfort,
        for they shall explore new lands.

Blessed are those who stay in for the long haul, those who
    turn the other cheek and don't turn back,
        for they shall be trusted.

Blessed are those who listen to the stories of our elders,
        for they will be respected.

Blessed are those who remember the ones who went
    before us in the struggle,
        for they are well grounded and will
        keep us real.

Blessed are the poor in spirit
        for they shall find joy,

Blessed are the humble listeners,
Blessed are those who live their faith as witnesses,
Blessed are those who take the words of Jesus seriously.
Blessed are the broken,
        for they shall become a new whole.

                        Nancy Peterson, November 2010

FAITH AND PRACTICE

PRACTICE

We meet together for common worship, for the pastoral care of our membership, for needful administration, for unhurried deliberation on matters of common concern, for testing personal concerns that are brought before us, and to get to know one another better in things that are eternal as in things that are temporal.

Quaker Faith & Practice, Britain Yearly Meeting of Friends, 1995, 3.02.

FAITH AND PRACTICE

Meeting for Worship

...I found myself one of a small company of silent worshipers, who were content to sit down together without words, that each one might feel after and draw near to the divine Presence unhindered at least, if not helped, by any human utterance. Utterance I knew was free, should the words be given; and before the meeting was over, a sentence or two were uttered in great simplicity...

My whole soul was filled with the unutterable peace of the undisturbed opportunity for communion with God, with the sense that at last I had found a place where I might, without the faintest suspicion of insincerity, join with others in simply seeking [the divine] Presence. Friends meetings have indeed been to me the greatest of outward help to a fuller and fuller entrance into the spirit from which they have sprung...
—Caroline Stephen, 1890. (1)

Centrality of Meeting for Worship

Worship is the central, unifying practice of our Quaker faith. Worship is an unmediated relationship of the Divine Presence with individuals and with the community. We wait together in silence to know this presence and respond to God's leadings and guidance for our individual lives and our life together. Listening for divine guidance is the core of Quaker worship. Through the direct experience of the sacred, whether we name it or leave it unnamed, we come to know the source of our being. We are linked to one another when we are brought together in the Light of the Spirit and are inspired to be creative in our own spiritual lives. Thomas Kelly wrote:

> *...in a gathered meeting, the sense is present that a new Life and Power has entered our midst...We are in communication with one another because we are being communicated to, and through, by the Divine Presence* (2)

As individuals we are unified in a body that worships God, sharing the gathered power of God's living presence.

Worship in Daily Life

God is present in all of life. We may become aware of the Presence and hear God's voice at any time and in any place. Meeting for worship happens at the specific time and place we set aside when we are prepared to come together as a community of faith in an atmosphere of expectant listening to hear the prompting of God. It is important that as individuals we prepare to hear and follow the guidance of the Spirit through personal worship, worship sharing in small groups, meditation, prayer study, and/or reading, as well as practicing other spiritual disciplines throughout the week, especially before meeting for worship. Participation in the meeting's work, study, singing, playing, and eating together also prepares us to worship as a body. The action and work that we are moved to take grow out of worship which further prepares us for worship.

Meeting for Worship

In Northern Yearly Meeting, most meetings for worship are unprogrammed. Some meetings have regular semi-programmed meetings for worship, which include planned music, scriptural and other readings, prayers, and spoken messages to support and surround the silence. A semi-programmed format is often used for celebrations and special events in the life of the community such as weddings and memorial services.

To set the proper tone, and out of consideration for all who enter, each of us is responsible for preparing ourselves for worship and taking our place in the meeting room before the stated time. If there is a study group or singing before worship, the clerk or other designated person will acknowledge the beginning of worship. Children often join us for short periods at the beginning and/or end of meeting for worship.

Unprogrammed worship begins in expectant, silent waiting, and listening. A sense of quiet and care of the whole community is observed, so that we may be unified in the Light.

As silence settles on the meeting, there comes a sense of our spiritual community and a vivid awareness of the ministry of silence. This is a ministry of being present to and for one another in the presence of God. It is a ministry of community and openness to the movements of the Divine Spirit in our lives. We seek and treasure the experience of a "gathered meeting"—one in which we are brought together in quiet communion and bonded in an awareness of God.

Meeting for worship usually lasts approximately one hour, but may be shorter or longer as determined by the leading of the Spirit. The clerk, or other designated person, closes the meeting for worship with a clasping of hands that is passed around the room. Some meetings hold hands in a circle. Additional reflections, introduction and announcements may follow.

Spoken Ministry During Meeting for Worship

A Quaker meeting for worship is more than the silence and waiting in the rich ministry of the Spirit. Promptings of God flowing through the silence lead to tender sharing of messages. This vocal ministry and careful listening are equally treasured elements of our worship. We willingly share "promptings of the spirit" out of the stillness. We wrap spoken ministry in a silence of its own, seeking a depth of understanding beyond the words and listening for the guidance of the Spirit in responding to the message.

Our meetings for worship go beyond private reverie. It is our experience that wherever two or more of us are gathered in expectant listening, the Spirit is in our midst. The quest for Truth among us is shared in community. We seek to be open to the call to provide vocal ministry. As individuals we do not initiate messages without clear prompting from the Spirit. When giving vocal ministry, we are asked to mind the Spirit, to keep close to the root of the message, to avoid unnecessary words, to speak clearly and distinctly so all can hear, and to allow time between messages for each message to be weighed carefully. Vocal ministry does not take the form of dialogue.

The meeting is gathered when messages come from the Divine so that when someone speaks it is what many others are experiencing. It is important for us to respect both the silence and the shared messages of our worshiping community.

Going Forth from Meeting for Worship

The practice of attending worship regularly leads us to a deeper relationship with the Divine and to a stronger Meeting community. It nurtures us in our spiritual journey whether as mature travelers or novices. Through worship, we can be transformed by the Spirit to be patterns and examples, wherever we are, so our lives speak to all people and they may be empowered to live their daily lives responding to that of God in all creation. Our worship leads to action. To paraphrase William Penn, experiencing Truth does not turn us out of the world, but enables us to live better in it and excites our endeavors to mend it. (3)

> ...for when I came into the silent assemblies of God's people, I felt a secret power among them, which touched my heart; and as I gave way unto it I found the evil weakening in me and the good raised up...
> — Robert Barclay, 1678. (4)

Queries

For individuals:

1. How do I center on the Divine Presence?
2. How do I enhance the gathered community?
3. Do I make meeting for worship a regular part of my spiritual practice?
4. Am I attentive to promptness?
5. Do I open myself to hearing the Divine in all messages?
6. Do I have a daily practice that assists me to be open to the Spirit?

For meetings:

1. How do we keep our meetings for worship centered with expectant waiting on the Divine?
2. How are Friends encouraged in their vocal ministry, through example and discussion, so that spiritual insights are shared and nurtured?
3. How do we teach our children the meaning and practice of worship?
4. Are meeting members attentive to the needs of others during worship?

5. How does our meeting assist Friends in preparing for worship?
6. How does our meeting help our members and attenders remove barriers to their attendance?

References:

1. Caroline Stephen, *Quaker Strongholds*, Passages Selected by Mary Gould Ogilvie (Pendle Hill Pamphlet no. 59, 1951), pp. 5–6.
2. Thomas Kelly, *The Gathered Meeting* [1944 edition] http://www.tractassociation.org/tracts/the-gathered-meeting/ (accessed 5 September 2016).
3. William Penn, *No Cross, No Crown* (1682), part 1, Ch.5, No. 12.
4. Robert Barclay, *Apology for the True Christian Divinity*, (1678), prop 11, sect. 7, p. 240.

Approved 2005

Decision Making

Friends, keep your meetings in the power of God...and in the love of God...and wait upon the Lord...
—George Fox, 1658. (1)

Friends conduct business together in the faith that there is one divine Spirit which is accessible to all persons; when Friends wait upon, heed and follow the Light of Truth within them, its Spirit will lead to unity. This faith is the foundation for any group decision...it is of prime importance that Friends understand and follow this procedure for business in the Monthly Meeting...[This] principle underlies all activities of the Society of Friends.
—North Pacific Yearly Meeting, 1986. (2)

Worship as the Basis

Friends make decisions based on the experience that the will of God can be discerned both individually and as a group. Regular worship as a faith community is an important foundation for that discernment. The Divine Spirit is active among us. Heeding the Light within can help us find unity in what we do. Thus our group decision-making occurs in a meeting for worship to conduct business.

History

Historically, groundwork was laid for the current method of making corporate decisions in the late 1650s in England. The meeting of Friends in Balby, Yorkshire, in 1656 wrote:

Dearly beloved Friends, These things we do not lay upon you as a rule or form to walk by, but that all, with a measure of light which is pure and holy may be guided; and so in the light walking and abiding, these things may be fulfilled in the Spirit, not in the letter; for the letter killeth but the Spirit giveth life.
—Meeting of Elders, 1656. (3)

Also at a general meeting at Skipton in 1659, Friends in the North wrote:

That the power of the God head may be known in the body...that none may exercise lordship or dominion over another, nor the person of any be set apart, but as they continue in the power of truth...that truth itself in the body may reign, not persons nor forms... (4)

George Fox established monthly, quarterly, and yearly meetings in England and America in the late 1660s and early 1670s. These meetings were established because the Society was in need of a means to check individual leadings against the larger group decisions and leadings. Initially, business meetings were for men only but separate women's business meetings began to appear as early as 1656, and George Fox urged that women's business meetings be established everywhere. By 1671 there was a business meeting in London including men and women. Today men and women participate equally in the decision making in the same meeting for worship for business.

Decision Making

The Monthly Meeting is the fundamental unit of the Religious Society of Friends. It consists of a group of Friends who meet together at regular intervals to wait upon God in Meeting for Worship and Meeting for Business.
—North Pacific Yearly Meeting, 1986. (5)

Conduct of the Business Meeting

The meeting for business begins with worship. Some meetings use this as an opportunity for worship sharing on a query or advice.

Those with agenda items let the clerk know in advance to allow proper placement of the items on the agenda. The clerk proposes the agenda, preferably publishing it in advance. He or she conducts the meeting, facilitating the discussion by drawing out those reticent to speak and encouraging others to share the time equitably. The clerk seeks expression of dissenting opinion, upholding the meeting in the Light throughout the process. The recording clerk or assistant clerk records the proceedings. The clerks discern and bring forth in words the sense of the meeting. At some point in a discussion the clerk may summarize his or her perception of the sense of the meeting for approval or further discussion. At times a member of the meeting may propose a minute, which attempts to summarize the sense of the meeting. When a decision is made, the recording clerk prepares and reads a minute, modifying it if needed for approval by the meeting.

Issues brought before the meeting are first clearly defined; then information is gathered, alternatives explored, and feelings and concerns expressed as the meeting moves toward decision. This process (studying an issue to seek the Light) Friends call seasoning. Seasoning of issues can be done in committee or by other means before the business meeting. The business meeting must resist the temptation to redo the work of committees, and the meeting must be open to new light in discussion of committee recommendations. Seasoning of agenda items before bringing them to the business meeting can help work out differences. Both the clerks and individual Friends have the responsibility to inform themselves about agenda items before the business meeting.

All present are responsible for the right working of the meeting for worship for business:

- maintaining a worshipful attitude;
- listening carefully to and being respectful of others;
- speaking when led, briefly, to the point and without repetition;
- addressing the clerk by standing or raising their hand when they wish to speak (depending on the size and custom of the meeting);
- not speaking to individuals;
- coming prepared and informed;
- seasoning matters by good committee work or other ways before bringing them to the meeting;
- coming with minds open to the working of the Spirit, being prepared to have their minds changed and setting personal interests aside;
- working towards unity when differences are present.

New truths may emerge along with new understandings as Friends seek to reach a decision.

In large meetings the clerk does not usually participate in the discussion. In small meetings the clerk often actively participates in the discussion. In either case the clerk steps aside as clerk if the subject is one where he or she has a conflict of interest, has strong opinions, or cannot be objective. In many meetings both members and attenders participate equally. If a person cannot be at a business meeting and wants an opinion shared, he or she may write a letter to the clerk to be read at business meeting. That person should understand that a letter is not a substitute for being present to hear the opinions of others and to sense the working of the Spirit. The clerk or anyone present may ask for silent worship at times of tension.

Business of the yearly meeting occurs at annual session and executive meetings with the same format and principles.

Unity, Sense of the Meeting, and Dealing with Serious Differences

Friends strive to know and follow God's will for our meeting life. They do not vote or use majority rule. Rather they seek the truth and unity of the Spirit. Discerning God's leading is both an individual and a communal process in which the meeting listens to each Friend and each Friend listens to the meeting. They accept a decision when they sense it is the will of God. When they listen to God and to each other, and achieve unity in our sense of God's leading, they are living in the Truth. They call this unity "the sense of the meeting."

Unity is found when all or nearly all those present believe that the proposed decision is truly Spirit led. If an objection is raised to a decision supported by most, the person or persons objecting may offer to stand aside to allow the meeting to proceed, sometimes asking to have the objection recorded. If the person or persons objecting do not wish to stand aside, Friends must devote the necessary time to prayerfully, thoughtfully, respectfully, and tenderly consider the objection. A threshing session may be called, or a special meeting with those objecting can be arranged to explore alternatives. Praying privately for guidance from the Spirit may be helpful. The person dissenting carries a special responsibility to listen to the group, to seek divine leading, and to work actively with others to seek alternatives.

After further consideration, if the objection remains, the meeting decides whether the weight of the objection will stop approval at this time, or whether the sense of the meeting will allow approval and moving forward despite the objection, or whether there is another way to proceed. If some members of the meeting are convinced the objection is grounded in a direct perception of God's will, the meeting is warned not to declare a sense of the meeting prematurely. The meeting seeks a balance—respecting the views of the dissenting persons, remembering that the dissenters may have a clearer knowledge of the truth. The meeting considers the weight of the objections and the judgment of the meeting as a whole. It is exceptional for one or a few individuals to block an action agreed upon by most. It is incumbent upon those objecting to listen carefully to the meeting, remembering that it is the leading and discernment of the meeting as a whole, which tests and validates the leading of individuals. Divine love is a binding force, and to experience that love in a meeting for business one must sometimes be willing to be bound by one's community.

On rare occasions, Friends can move forward with decisions which are not unanimous but which still express the sense of the meeting. Major decisions among Friends on issues of abolition of slave holding and women's rights were sometimes minuted despite objection. However, proceeding with a decision over the objection of some risks losing members or even splitting the meeting. Where there is no clear sense of the meeting, the decision can be laid aside or postponed and put on the agenda for another meeting for worship for business. A particular challenge to the meeting community exists when differences exist on an issue where a decision is urgent and cannot be postponed.

Threshing Sessions

For decisions that are controversial or that require additional time, the clerk or the meeting may call for a threshing session. A threshing session is a meeting where everyone is encouraged to express their views but with no intention of coming to a decision. Ultimately unity is best reached if full opportunity is given for differences to be aired and faced, and a threshing session is just such an opportunity. Threshing sessions also give opportunity for background information to be reviewed.

A Called Meeting for Business

At times a decision will be of such importance and will take up such a large amount of time that a special meeting for worship for business will be called devoted to one topic. The purpose of this meeting for worship for business will be to reach a decision if possible. A called meeting for worship for business should be announced and publicized well in advance so that all will have the opportunity to attend

Conclusion

The Quaker corporate decision making process is a spiritual discipline needing trust, patience, a willingness to listen, mutual forbearance, a concern for and openness to others with differing views, and the grace of humor. The care with which we conduct our decision-making is often critical to the enduring harmony of the entire meeting. At its best the result reflects the transforming power of the love of God, an exhilarating and joyful experience.

Queries

1. Are meetings in which business is conducted held in a spirit of worship?
2. Do we seek truth and the right course of action, rather than acceptance of a previously formed opinion?
3. Do we maintain a spirit of love, patience, and understanding?
4. Do we help one another in our search for unity by speaking briefly and without repetition?
5. Are we tender and considerate of our differing views?
6. Do we recognize that the will of God can at times be more clearly perceived by an individual or by the minority rather

than the majority and that careful attention must be given to minority discernment as a valid channel of the will of God?

References:

1. George Fox, *Epistle 162*, 1658.
2. North Pacific Yearly Meeting, *Faith and Practice*, 1993, p. 56.
3. Britain Yearly Meeting, *Quaker Faith and Practice,* 1995, 1.01 "Letter from Friends in Balby": *Letters Etc. of Early Friends,* p. 282.
4. Howard Brinton, *Friends for 300 Years*, "Letter from Friends in Skipton," Wallingford, PA: Pendle Hill Publications, 1994, p. 100
5. North Pacific Yearly Meeting, p. 52.

Approved 1999

Yearly Meeting Structure and Function

Recognizing the joy and celebration experienced each time we gather together for fellowship and as a worshiping community, individual Friends and Friends within several monthly meetings in the Wisconsin-Minnesota area announce the birth of a new entity within the Religious Society of Friends: Northern Yearly Meeting

In drawing together, we subscribe to what earlier Friends wrote about the nature of a yearly meeting: it "shall be a free association of Monthly Meetings for mutual support and consultation and for furthering such concerns as its members have in common. Its relation to a Monthly Meeting is consultative and not authoritative."
—Northern Yearly Meeting, 1975. (1)

From the minute establishing Northern Yearly Meeting, September 14, 1975, Frontenac, *Minnesota.*

When ye are met in the Light...hearken to it, that ye may feel the Power of God in every one of you..."
—George Fox, 1656 (2)

Faith and Practice

Yearly Meeting is a place in the rocks where the Spirit bursts forth...and we can come and drink of it.
—Rosalie Wahl, 2002. (3)

Northern Yearly Meeting meets in an annual session, and in such interim sessions as may be needed, to worship in the manner of Friends, to practice corporate discernment under the guidance of the Spirit as we conduct our business, to celebrate and to share our lives and work as a community of Friends. Through meetings for worship for business we aspire to model Friendly decision-making, seeking clarity, unity, and obedience to the One who guides us. We share news of and participate in the lives of monthly meetings and worship groups, and our regional and national Quaker organizations. We learn the many ways in which our brothers and sisters in the Society of Friends give life to their faith, and we rededicate ourselves to the task of giving legs to our own faith and making it walk upon the earth.

We celebrate our time together with song, enjoyment of nature, play, and by breaking bread together. We share our spiritual journeys and Friendly concerns with worship sharing, workshops, interest groups, and plenary sessions. We live in community for a few days with children and adults of all ages. We struggle together with difficult and sometimes painful issues. We sometimes disagree but often see the Spirit at work as we unite in a sense of the meeting over those disagreements. We sense the dedication and hard work of many people to live our Quaker testimonies, to make the Yearly Meeting run, and to care for our children and youth. At times we truly feel the Power of God at work and the Spirit bursting forth. Those are precious and inspiring moments. We seek to find a balance between the varied manifestations of our faith, the numerous creative activities to which they give rise, and at the same time maintain simplicity in our schedule. We come away with our faith challenged, deepened, inspired, and renewed.

Yearly Meeting Structure and Function

Northern Yearly Meeting (NYM) is comprised of monthly meetings, preparative meetings, and worship groups, mainly from Wisconsin and Minnesota, with some from upper Michigan, Iowa, North and South Dakota. Each of those meetings designates a representative to the Yearly Meeting. These designated representatives communicate the activities of NYM to their meetings and the concerns of their meeting to NYM. All Friends are encouraged to participate in this work for the mutual support and consultation of NYM member meetings and for furthering such concerns as its member meetings have in common.

Within Northern Yearly Meeting, the monthly meeting is the fundamental unit of the religious Society of Friends. These meetings carry the primary responsibility of membership, oversight of marriages, and sustaining the ongoing life of the worship community. Northern Yearly Meeting also includes many small groups of Friends who gather as worship groups. They may seek affiliation with a larger meeting for assistance and support. A worship group may become a preparative meeting, when appropriate, under the care of a monthly meeting. There are also a number of isolated Friends in our region who participate in Yearly Meeting annual sessions and others activities. Northern Yearly Meeting also includes a variety of regional gatherings meeting at times other than annual session for worship and fellowship. Young adult friends, in particular, have fully participated in the yearly meeting even when not worshiping with a local meeting community.

All Friends are invited and encouraged to attend the Yearly Meeting annual session and the interim sessions, to become active in the work of the Yearly Meeting, to enjoy the fellowship and perspective of the wider family of friends in our region, and to cherish the mutual blessings of worship, witness, and community.

New Gatherings of Friends in Northern Yearly Meeting

We are concerned that all who are moved to worship after the manner of Friends may be able to do so. In areas where no Friends meetings exist, we encourage individual Friends and those drawn to Friends' ways to meet together and seek Divine guidance.

An established Meeting may find that it has grown so large or that some of its members live at such a distance from the meeting place that it becomes desirable to form a Meeting in a new place. Such a gathering may start as a worship group or preparative meeting.

Worship Groups

A worship group is a gathering of persons who meet regularly for worship after the manner of Friends and desire to be identified with the principles and practices of the Religious Society of Friends. Such a group may originate independently or be formed by a monthly meeting for the convenience of its members living in a certain area. A worship group usually names one person to serve as a convenor and correspondent of the group. Such a group may wish to relate itself to an established monthly meeting and come under its regular counsel and care. Worship groups do not receive members, hold weddings, or otherwise act formally as an established monthly meeting. Such actions are done through a monthly meeting to which appropriate application may be made.

If a worship group feels that it is ready to organize and conduct its own business in the manner of an established meeting, it may consider becoming a preparative meeting under the care of a monthly meeting, or it may feel ready to apply for monthly meeting status in Northern Yearly Meeting without first becoming a preparative meeting. Great care and deliberation at this time may prevent complications later.

Yearly Meeting Structure and Function

Preparative Meetings

A preparative meeting is a meeting for worship and for business, which is under the care of and reports regularly to a monthly meeting and that ordinarily, looks forward to becoming a monthly meeting. A preparative meeting has officers and committees as needed, after the manner of a monthly meeting, and should hold a business meeting once a month. It should have the continuing care and counsel of a committee of oversight selected by the sponsoring monthly meeting. A preparative meeting does not receive members, hold weddings, or otherwise act formally as an established meeting; such actions, if desired by a preparative meeting, are brought to and carried out through an appropriate monthly meeting. Memberships in a preparative meeting are held by the monthly meeting to which it is related.

New Monthly Meetings

When a worship group or a preparative meeting feels it is ready to become a monthly meeting, application requesting aid in the process shall be made to the Yearly Meeting or one of the monthly meetings. If it seems right and timely for this organization to take place, the Yearly or monthly meeting shall appoint a clearness committee to meet with the applicant meeting. If application is made to the Yearly Meeting, the clerk(s) of Northern Yearly Meeting in consultation with the clerk(s) of Advancement and Outreach Committee, and the applicant meeting shall appoint the clearness committee, which shall have from five to eight members. The clearness committee should continue oversight of the new meeting for one year following its recognition. (A monthly meeting may form a clearness committee according to its good order. It is urged to observe the following process as well as the Yearly Meeting committee.)

FAITH AND PRACTICE

Application Process

The functions of the Northern Yearly Meeting clearness committee are to meet with the applicant meeting at its location, to assess its readiness, to answer such questions as its members have, to provide support and counsel as needed, and to make a recommendation at the following Yearly Meeting session. The following points are suggested for consideration.

Application: The meeting should submit in writing to the Northern Yearly Meeting clerk(s) a statement telling why it wishes to become a monthly meeting and why it feels it may be ready for this step. In preparing this statement the applicant meeting should consider the following questions.

History and Experience: How long has it been meeting? What geographical area does it serve? Where and when is its meeting for worship? What is the usual attendance? How many Friends, other attenders and children are there in the meeting? Of those taking responsibility for the meeting, how many appear well settled in the area? Is there vitality in the meeting for worship? What are the meeting's social concerns? How are the needs of various populations within the meeting met?

Evidence of Good Order: Is the meeting acquainted with Friends' principles and practices? Has the meeting studied various books of Faith and Practice? What officers are in place? Are the functions of the clerk and officers understood? What committees does it have? Are financial matters being handled in an orderly manner? Are plans being made for minuted record keeping of memberships, births, deaths, and marriages?

Obligations to the Yearly Meeting: The Clearness Committee shall discuss with the applicant meeting the obligations of membership in Northern Yearly Meeting. These include serving on committees and contributing financially.

Upon recommendation to and approval of the application by Northern Yearly Meeting, the new meeting is recognized as an independent monthly meeting and a member of Northern Yearly Meeting. Then a specific time and place shall be set for the organization of the new monthly meeting. Members of the clearness committee are encouraged to be present and offer counsel if needed.

Affiliation Process for Other Friends Meetings

Other Friends worship groups or established monthly meetings wishing to form ties with Northern Yearly Meeting may do so by submitting a letter of application. The clerks of Northern Yearly Meeting in consultation with the clerk(s) of the Advancement and Outreach Committee and the applicant meeting shall appoint a clearness committee. The functions of the clearness committee shall be to meet with the applicant group at its own location, discuss the meaning and responsibilities of membership in the Yearly Meeting, answer questions, and provide support and counsel as needed. A recommendation shall be presented at the next session of the yearly meeting. Upon positive action, the group will become a member of Northern Yearly Meeting.

Friends groups and isolated Friends are welcome to participate in the various functions of Northern Yearly Meeting regardless of formal affiliation.

Northern Yearly Meeting Finances

Friends do not take collections or ask for money during meeting for worship. Each monthly meeting, preparative meeting, and worship group is encouraged to contribute to support the work of the Yearly Meeting. Historically the Yearly Meeting has suggested a dollar amount the constituent meetings are asked to give for each of their regular members and attenders. Individuals are also encouraged to contribute separately as led. At the Yearly Meeting annual session and at other times we may be asked and moved to contribute to special causes or Friends organizations.

Officers and Committees

Northern Yearly Meeting has officers and committees that carry out the work of the Yearly Meeting. The Nominating Committee has a detailed job description for each position, which includes gifts or qualifications of individuals filling the positions along with responsibilities and activities of the position. Since the job descriptions are lengthy and dynamic, those descriptions are not included here, but can be obtained from the Nominating Committee.

Officers, committee members and clerks, and representatives to Quaker organizations are nominated by the Nominating Committee and are subject to approval of the body at annual session. The exceptions to this practice are Nominating Committee, whose members and clerk are named by the Naming Committee; and Naming Committee members, whose members are identified by the Clerk.

Officers

   Clerk (or Presiding Clerk)
   Assistant Clerk
   Recording Clerk
   Treasurer
   Archivist

Standing Committees

   Advancement and Outreach
   Annual Sessions Planning

Yearly Meeting Structure and Function

Finance
Children and Youth
Communications
Faith and Practice
Ministry and Nurture
Nominating
Naming
Peace and Social Concerns
NYM/El Salvador

Representatives to Quaker Organizations

The following organizations have requested representatives from Yearly Meetings as part of their governance. Northern Yearly Meeting endeavors to fill the positions that have been allocated to us.

American Friends Service Committee
Friends Committee on National Legislation
Friends General Conference
Friends World Committee for Consultation
Friends for Lesbian, Gay, Bisexual, Transgender, and
    Queer Concerns
Quaker Earthcare Witness
Scattergood School

See Appendices

Appendix A - Original Minute Establishing Northern
    Yearly Meeting
Appendix B - Why Develop a Faith and Practice

References:

1. Northern Yearly Meeting, *The Minutes of Northern Yearly*

Meeting of the Religious Society of Friends, September 14, 1975, Frontenac, Minnesota.
2. George Fox, , Epistle 130, 1656.
3. Rosalie Wahl,. Northern Yearly Meeting Executive Committee, held at Menominee, Wisconsin, used with verbal permission of speaker to member of Faith and Practice Committee, October 4, 2002.

Approved 2006, Revised 2015

Membership

When we consider the criteria for membership, the two greatest factors are community and commitment. Not just a practical commitment, but a spiritual willingness to grow and learn, out of which practical commitment will evolve.
— A group of Young English Friends, 1986. (1)

Definition of Membership

A member is a person who is recorded as a member by a monthly meeting. Membership actions are minuted in the official minutes of the monthly meeting.

Membership in the Religious Society of Friends is meant to be a joyful responsibility in a community that is intended to enrich the spiritual journey of all.

Members belong to and represent their local and yearly meeting and the Religious Society of Friends. As members, we affirm our concurrence with the testimonies and practices of the Society and our willingness to do our best to live by them. Membership is an acknowledgment of willingness to contribute to the life of the meeting.

Our seeking and discerning the leadings of the Spirit occur within the unique tradition of the Religious Society of Friends. We maintain openness to continuing revelation but are willing to compare our leadings with those of others within the context of the Religious Society of Friends, both historic and current.

We believe that all are called to minister in some capacity. It is the responsibility of each member to contribute to the life of the meeting and of the Society of Friends as the Spirit leads. All Friends are open to hearing and answering their individual call to service. It is important for Friends to participate with their worshipful presence in meeting for worship and in meeting for worship for business. Ministry takes many forms. This may include, but is not limited to, spoken ministry, serving on committees, holding offices, providing financial support, teaching First Day School, leading discussions, joining in adult religious education, participating in the activities of the meeting and wider Quaker organizations, representing the meeting to other organizations, supporting others in their efforts, and caring for others.

Membership does not imply that one has reached a particular level of spirituality. Membership is an acknowledgment of a person's desire to contribute to a meeting in a deeper way and in return an acknowledgment by the meeting that the deepening of its relationship with the individual is welcomed with joy. All members continue to seek the Truth and remain open to continuing revelation. It is an active commitment to the process of spiritual growth.

Practice

Membership is determined by each monthly meeting.

Recording of Membership

Memberships are recorded and held within a monthly meeting. In worship groups and preparative meetings, formal membership is held with the parent meeting. A member of a monthly meeting within Northern Yearly Meeting also holds membership in Northern Yearly Meeting.

Membership

Becoming a Member

Adults:

An individual may apply for membership in a particular monthly meeting. This is done by attenders and by associate members who wish to continue as members.

Children:

A child may be recorded as either a birthright or associate member. This can be done at birth, or adoption, or later. To do so, the parent(s) or guardian(s) make a written request to the meeting requesting membership for the child under their care. If it is approved, the membership status is recorded by the monthly meeting.

Associate:

An associate member is a child of a member of a monthly meeting. This person is to make a decision on continuing membership at the age of discernment. Either the associate member or the monthly meeting may initiate this process.

Convincement:

Convinced Friends are those who have determined that their spiritual path is nurtured by membership in the Religious Society of Friends and who have been accepted into membership by a monthly meeting. Becoming a member by convincement is not something to be rushed, nor should people be pushed into becoming members.

Birthright:

A birthright Friend is a child who is born or adopted into the family of a recorded member of a monthly meeting. The child is recorded as a full member. Some meetings within Northern Yearly Meeting recognize birthright status, but most do not.

While one may initially be drawn to the Religious Society of Friends by a particular aspect of our faith or practice, the person requesting membership will have moved beyond this to an understanding of the Society as a spiritual community. It is expected that this person will have experienced meeting for worship and meeting for worship for business over a period of time. It is also expected that prospective members will have some understanding of Quaker faith, worship, practices, manner of conducting business, and the meaning of membership. Familiarity with the history and current work of the Society helps people in their decision concerning membership. It is hoped that the individual already feels a sense of belonging to the meeting community.

The prospective member applies for membership by writing a letter to the clerk of the meeting or appropriate committee such as Ministry and Counsel. The letter states an interest in membership and the basic reasons for which membership is being requested. A prospective member is encouraged to consult with the clerk or with other Friends when considering the implications of membership.

The clerk or appropriate committee member may read the letter of application at the next meeting for worship for business. In many meetings, a clearness committee for membership will be formed at that time. If the process is the responsibility of a committee, the letter might not be brought to meeting for worship for business until the clearness process is complete. Some meetings may have a standing committee for the clearness process.

The clearness committee for membership consists of two or more members of the meeting. If the prospective member attends a worship group or preparative meeting, that group should be represented on the committee along with members of the parent meeting.

The clearness committee will meet with the prospective member one or more times over the following months. It is the responsibility of this committee to worshipfully seek assurance that the person applying for membership has been divinely led to this point, has an understanding of and desire to live by the princi-

Membership

ples of Friends, and that this person's way of continued seeking is compatible with the manner of Friends. The clearness process is an opportunity for deep spiritual sharing and an opportunity for all participants to grow in their understanding and their faith.

After careful deliberation, the clearness committee will recommend:

- The individual is ready for membership, or
- More time is needed before moving forward.

The recommendation of the clearness committee is brought to meeting for worship for business, either directly or through the parent committee. Some meetings may delay the decision another month for seasoning. If there are reservations about accepting the recommendation for membership, concerns will be expressed and the clearness committee will again meet with the person who has applied for membership. Friends with concerns have a responsibility to express them and may be invited to this meeting.

If the membership is approved at a meeting for business, the person requesting membership is recorded as a member. This person is welcomed into the community as a member.

A meeting may have a welcoming process for all new members.

Some monthly meetings require membership in order for a person to serve in some positions.

Transfer of Membership

Individuals who wish to transfer their membership to a different monthly meeting or religious community shall write a letter to their original meeting stating the request. If it is approved, the clerk writes a letter to the new meeting or religious community advising them of the transfer and referring the member to its care.

When receiving a request for a transfer into a monthly meeting, the meeting may act immediately, or it may establish a clearness committee. The clearness process is an opportunity to build community with the new member.

Sojourner

Sojourners are members of a monthly meeting other than that which they are attending. A limited period of stay in the visited monthly meeting makes transfer of membership inappropriate. They are recognized as sojourners by a letter from the clerk of their home meeting to the clerk of the monthly meeting that they are attending.

Termination of Membership

A person may come to understand that membership in the Religious Society of Friends is no longer appropriate. The individual formally requests termination of membership in a letter addressed to the clerk or a member of an appropriate committee will read the letter at the next meeting for worship for business. If there are no unresolved issues, the resignation will be honored. If there are unresolved issues, the meeting may ask the individual to participate in a clearness committee.

Monthly meetings may remove inactive members from the membership roll. Prior to termination of membership, all reasonable effort will be made to contact the individual. If no response is received or if they state that they no longer feel a call to membership in the meeting, their membership is laid down by approval at a meeting for worship for business.

Recorded members, who act contrary to the life of the meeting, may be removed from formal membership. This action will not be undertaken lightly. Prayerful consideration will be given. Conscientious effort is made to understand the individual's current situation and attitude about the meeting and to restore that person to the community. This may take the form of a clearness committee in which the individual is encouraged to participate.

Membership

The committee will then bring its recommendations to meeting for worship for business, where the formal decision will be made.

When membership is terminated, it is recorded by the meeting.

Members Who Are Geographically Distant From Their Monthly Meetings

Some Friends move away from their home meeting but feel that the monthly meeting where their membership is recorded is still their spiritual home. They have an active desire to retain membership in that meeting. This desire may be honored. These people and their home meetings actively maintain communication. However, Friends who move away are encouraged to seek out community in a meeting in their new locale when one exists.

Attenders

An attender is one who does not have a formal membership status in any monthly meeting, but who is drawn to worship with and share in the life of a meeting. Meetings are encouraged to be attentive to frequent attenders and to encourage them in becoming formal members, as they feel led.

Queries

For individuals:

1. What does it mean to me to be a member of the Religious Society of Friends?
2. To what extent are my beliefs consistent with the testimonies and practices of Friends? How do they differ?
3. What are my reservations about being a Friend?
4. What do I expect from the Religious Society of Friends, this yearly meeting, and this monthly meeting/preparative meeting/worship group as it relates to my life and spiritual growth?

5. In what ways can I contribute to the life of the Society of Friends? To this yearly meeting? To this monthly meeting/preparative meeting/worship group?
6. How prepared am I to be a minister and spokesperson for the Religious Society of Friends? How well do I represent the Religious Society of Friends in my daily life and activities?

For meetings:

1. How do the yearly meeting and the local meetings promote the spiritual growth and development of its members?
2. In what ways does our meeting provide opportunities for attenders to deepen their knowledge of the Religious Society of Friends?
3. In what way does our Quaker community reach out to those seeking a spiritual home?
4. How do clearness committees for membership hold to the discipline of respect for those seeking membership?
5. How do committees for membership listen for the meaning of words that the applicant uses?
6. Is sufficient attention given to maintain the confidentiality for all committee conversations?
7. What means does our meeting have of welcoming new members?

References:

1. A group of Young Friends, 1986. *Young Quaker*, Vol. 32, #4, p. 1-2. As quoted in *Quaker Faith and Practice*, Britain Yearly Meeting, 1994. 10.25.

Approved 2001, Queries revised 2015

Marriage

Then in the marriage union, the independence of husband and wife will be equal, their dependence mutual, and their obligations reciprocal.
—Lucretia Coffin Mott, 1849. (1)

A [couple] whose love for each other is part of their love for God discover a more splendid love and a more exuberant life than those who love each other only. The romantic molasses on which our [popular cultures] feed is a poor substitute for the nourishing food of God's love.
—Kenneth Boulding, 1942. (2)

Marriage joins two people in Divine care and an ongoing relationship to fully share their lives. We believe this union is something not lightly entered into, as it is a planned lifelong commitment. Marriage brings two unique individuals into a new entity, one of joy, grace, respect, and care for the other. The challenges of marriage, and sometimes the pains of it, provide the opportunity to grow into wholeness of life together with Divine guidance.

Several individual monthly meetings within Northern Yearly Meeting have prepared minutes affirming marriage regardless of sexual orientation. One of the earliest is:

Twin Cities Friends Meeting, joyfully recognizing the diversity of sexual orientation within our religious commu-

nity, affirms the goodness of committed, loving relationships that endure, are unselfish, and that provide mutual support and tenderness...We intend to follow the same customary and careful process of arriving at clearness for any couple, regardless of sexual orientation, who should wish to unite under our care...
—Twin Cities Friends Meeting, 1986. (3)

Our yearly meeting comes together in this affirmation with the following minute:

Our experience confirms that all people are equal before God and equally loved by God. In witnessing the truth of God's love to the wider community, we support full and equal inclusion of gays and lesbians in enjoying the rights and privileges afforded any citizen.
—Northern Yearly Meeting, 2006. (4)

Only monthly meetings have the authority to conduct marriage under the care of the meeting. Worship groups and preparative meetings may participate in the clearness process and planning for a marriage as members of their monthly meeting committee. Marriage under the care of a meeting celebrates publicly the couples' commitment to God, each other, and the meeting. Decisions regarding marriage are unique to each monthly meeting. Most monthly meetings do not accept care of a marriage unless one of the couple is already a member or an associate member of that monthly meeting.

The Clearness Process

This process begins when the couple sends a letter to the monthly meeting to request marriage under the care of that meeting. The letter is read at the next monthly meeting for worship for business, and a clearness committee is appointed to meet with the

Marriage

couple. Clearness committees explore the meeting's willingness to take on the care of the marriage. They also enhance a couple's preparation for marriage by helping them think about their commitment to each other at a deep level as well as the many practical issues they face. Some meetings have prepared materials for the clearness committee to use, which include care for the readiness of both individuals to be married and their clearness about being married within the Friends meeting for worship. (See Clearness Committees for Marriage, p. 104)

The same clearness process would be followed for all committed couples that have requested marriage under the care of a meeting. Now, and historically, legal and religious definitions of the marriage relationship are not always one and the same. A meeting clearness committee, as part of the preparations for marriage, may help a couple more carefully determine the characterization of their relationship.

The Wedding

The clearness committee brings its report to a meeting for worship for business. After meeting approves, an arrangements committee is appointed to work with the couple on the details of the wedding. In keeping with our testimony of simplicity, arrangement committees are encouraged to help couples focus the wedding plans on the deep spiritual nature of this union and the real lifelong commitment being made. This may include consideration of the differing beliefs and special needs of some families.

Arrangement committees should be cognizant of their state laws regarding marriage and provide clear information to the couple, so that all legal requirements, if applicable, are met in a timely manner. Friends are reminded that states vary in the marriage law requirements. If civil marriage recording is desired, state laws must be checked, usually with the county clerk's office. Direct the couple to contact the marriage license bureau four to six weeks before the appointed marriage date. The couple should be certain to inquire what official signatures and documents, including how many witnesses are needed on the license for a Quaker wedding. States may have specific requirements to handling name changes if such are desired.

The wedding itself is a called meeting for worship, which has the purpose and joy of supporting and witnessing the couple as they join their lives. No third person officiates at the wedding because we believe it is the Divine Spirit that gives this relationship life and permanence. During worship, the couple rises and speak their vows to each other. The traditional vow is: "In the presence of God and these our friends, I take thee, _____, to be my wife/husband/partner, promising with Divine assistance to be unto thee a loving and faithful wife/husband/partner as long as we both shall live." Other wordings may also be used. The vows should be words the couple truly can to commit to one another and desire to make. Clearness committees may assist couples in selecting the words they will say. Some couples choose to exchange rings.

The marriage certificate is an integral part of a Quaker wedding. Many couples experience the presence of their certificate in their family as a wonderful affirmation of the Divine blessing that brought them together and a reminder of the vows they said. Historically, civil authorities did not recognize Quaker weddings. So Friends developed the marriage certificate to provide the complete record of this event. (See Appendix C for sample wording for marriage certificates.)

The marriage certificate must be fully lettered before the wedding so that the couple may sign it during the wedding after they have said their vows. The certificate includes the words of the vows. Each should sign with the full name they plan to use from that date forward. A designated person then reads the entire certificate aloud during the wedding. All present are requested to sign the certificate as witnesses, at the rise of meeting for worship.

Historically, after the wedding, the entire wording of the marriage certificate and all of the witnesses' names were copied into a record book of the monthly meeting. Both the meeting and the couple retained this document. Today, it is more common for the meeting to record the event, but not record the entire certificate.

Continuing Care

The meeting's interest in a couple does not cease when the wedding event is concluded. The meeting is also to provide ongoing nurture and celebration of couples and families. This community can be the fertile spiritually nourishing ground where a marriage relationship can continue to unfold in the Light. The interested community may welcome the observation of special anniversaries by assisting with a meeting for worship for an anniversary. Meeting couples who were not married in the manner of Friends might even request a meeting for worship for the further affirmation and deepening of their vows. A meeting may provide assistance when a family experiences health problems or loss. It may formalize support to couples by sponsoring couple enrichment workshops and ongoing couple support groups. Couples within a meeting provide a model of rich Quaker marriage relationships as one kind of support to those considering marriage.

Continuing care may require times of providing counseling and clearness committees when families face difficulties. Many meetings experience gaps of awareness and awkwardness regarding ways to offer care. A meeting may want to locate friendly outside counseling and support services. Clearness committees may be offered to a couple considering divorce or separation, if they are open to that. A meeting can assist with the on-going nurture and care of any children that may be involved. The meeting community seeks to love and respect both of the individuals involved, and if possible, to help them continue to participate in the spiritual life of the meeting.

The On-going Union

Marriage can illuminate the spiritual journey with God for both the couple and the meeting community. The wholeness of a marriage seems to strengthen and multiply the gifts each is able to offer as individuals and that both are able to offer as a couple. Successful relationships give the meeting community a precious gift, a tangible model of the hard work and deep joy that true intimacy with self, others and God can bring.

Queries

For couples:

1. How will you, as future marriage partners, continue to seek The Light as you make decisions for your home and your family?
2. If your marriage is not legally recognized by your state, how will you protect and care for each other and any children?
3. What level of counseling and support would you, as a couple, feel free to seek from your meeting for continuing growth, or if difficulties are encountered?
4. How will you continue your relationship with your marriage clearness committee?
5. What is the couple's responsibility to the spiritual life of the meeting?

For meetings:

1. How does our meeting nurture the marriage commitment before the wedding?
2. How does our meeting help a couple come to clearness
3. How does our meeting and its clearness committees nurture the on-going relationship?

Marriage

4. How do our clearness committees and arrangements committees assist the couple to develop their vows and plan a wedding which will focus on the deep spiritual nature of the commitment and keep the celebration welcoming, orderly, and simple?
5. What does it mean to our meeting to support a marriage under the care of the meeting?
6. In what ways does our meeting offer assistance and support to couples who may encounter difficulties?
7. How will our meeting lovingly embrace both members of a couple if there is separation or divorce?
8. How does our meeting nurture and support all couples?
9. How does our meeting continue to nurture couples who move away from the meeting.
10. If a marriage under the care of the meeting is not legally recognized by the state, how will our meeting assist the couple to protect and care for each other and any children?

References:

1. *Lucretia Mott Speaking*, compiled by Margaret Hope Bacon (Pendle Hill Pamphlet #234, 1980), p. 14.
2. Kenneth Boulding, "The Practice of the Love of God," William Penn Lecture, 1942, p. 21-22, as quoted in *Faith and Practice*, Philadelphia Yearly Meeting, 1972, p. 107.
3. Twin Cities Friends Meeting, *The Minutes of the Twin Cities Friends Meeting*, October, 1986.
4. Northern Yearly Meeting, *The Minutes of the Northern Yearly Meeting of the Religious Society of Friends*, May 2006.

See Appendix

Appendix C: Marriage Certificates, Possible Wording

Approved 2008, Revised 2014

Clearness Committees for Marriage

These are possible questions that may help a clearness committee for marriage as it meets with a couple. None of them are required. The most important role of the Clearness Committee for marriage is to allow the Spirit to work within the group, as they are preparing for their meetings and as they meet. Couples need to know that there are no right or wrong answers to questions and that questions are raised to help reach clearness about whether a marriage should occur, whether it should occur within the meeting community, and what the specifics of the relationship will be. The questions are mostly derived from materials prepared by several monthly meetings within Northern Yearly Meeting, including Madison, Twin Cities, Minneapolis, and Prospect Hill as well as individual comments from Friends.

Clearness Queries for Marriage

For individuals:

1. How would you describe what an ideal, committed relationship might be?
2. How did you become acquainted with each other?
3. Are there differences in your backgrounds? How will these affect your relationship?
4. Have you shared gritty experiences as well as festive ones? Have you encountered each other when you were "not at your best?"
5. Often it is the little everyday things that can really build up and bug a person. To consider these things, do you put the cap back on the toothpaste, or leave it about? Do you want all of the dishes washed immediately after a meal, or whenever someone has time? What happens to your shoes when you

Marriage

arrive home? Do both of you take time to care for your home environment?

6. Are you a morning person or an evening person?

Families:

7. Why do you want to marry HIM/HER? Why do you want to MARRY him/her? Have both of you become acquainted with the extended families of each other? Are your families supporting your desire to marry? If not, how will that affect your relationship?

Spiritual:

8. Why do you want to be married under the care of the meeting? Do you seek to be an ongoing part of the meeting community? Do you feel that a spiritual community will support the spiritual life of your marriage?
9. Do you regard marriage as a sacred relationship? How will the "presence of God" be part of your home after the wedding ceremony?
10. What part do you expect marriage to play in your individual spiritual lives?
11. If you are not both Friends, how do you expect to reconcile your different spiritual practices? How will religious holidays be observed in your home? If there are children, which religion will they be raised in?

Futures and Responsibilities:

12. Have you considered the legal issues of marriage, the rights and responsibilities including disposition of property, financial issues, survivorship options?
13. Have you considered, as a couple, how you will manage your

money? How you will finance your home? Do you have the same ideas about lifestyle?
14. Have you discussed having children? If you have children from a previous relationship, how are you caring for their needs now? How will they be a part of your family after you marry?
15. If you cannot or choose not to obtain legal recognition of your marriage, have you made appropriate legal arrangements to the extent possible that protect you and any children?
16. Do both of you become involved when large decisions are to be made? If you do not initially agree, how are your differences resolved?
17. Is there anything you cannot talk about so far in your relationship? Do you think this interferes with the wholeness of your relationship?
18. Will you be a two-career family? How will you make changes if a new, better, different job is considered?
19. Do health requirements or physical and mental conditions raise concerns for you in this relationship? What if one of you becomes impaired?
20. What are you going to do, as your parents grow older?

For meetings:

21. Are we ready, as a meeting, to be a part of this relationship? To receive the care of this marriage?

Spiritual Nurture of Children within the Meeting Community

Let the little children come to me...For the Kingdom of God belongs to such as these.
—Luke 18:17 (NIV)

[My son Lowell] has forever convinced me that God is as real to the child as visible objects are...I am convinced that children have a sense of Presence in these times of intense community hush.
—Rufus Jones, 1947. (1)

We know that children often have experiences, which an adult might define as worship or prayer, before the child can say in words that that was the experience. Watch a child pause and just look and maybe wonder. Watch the child's eyes express this connecting to something beyond physical feelings. Allow each child the time and space to just be. Our children can invite and welcome us into their world of wonder, a world that our adult minds, possibly more rational, often skip over. Our children minister to us as they make discoveries.

Our teens inform us that gathering for meeting for worship feels much more possible when we know and trust everyone who joins us in the worshiping community. They also remind us that active preparation and clear intentions help us participate in worship. This is something that we demonstrate almost unconsciously by where we seat ourselves and how carefully we arrange our arrival time. It is very helpful to state this clear intention to our younger participants. (2)

Meetings carry much responsibility to be attentive in creating a sheltering environment and presence, which will offer welcome and build community for all. This may include times of intergenerational programming to help draw the community into worship. Individuals and families bring the responsibility of their own discipline of preparation, anticipation and participation.

A strong attribute of Quakerism is that our children are engaged and valued in the community work of the Spirit from birth onward. Children once learned what it meant to be Quaker simply by daily experiencing their own families, neighbors, and friends living their testimonies of simplicity, integrity, peace and equality. Today, our children do not often observe us during our work or our community activities. Nevertheless, we understand that we transmit our faith, our values, and our testimonies most completely through sharing real experiences with each other. Every meeting, at every stage of its experience, finds its own ways of connecting in loving community, beyond carefully nurturing the times set aside for worship. The Meeting becomes a source of grounding for all.

Northern Yearly Meeting annual session is the time where we come together for consultation, for nurture, and for immersion in the wider community of Quakers. Once here, we all are engaged in whatever work, play, business, sorrow, joy, sunshine or stormy weather we encounter. Together we practice listening to each other; we demonstrate spiritual discipline; we worship; we shout and romp and rejoice in the life of our community. We discover that this is a safe place to practice all of our Quakerly quirks. We have learned that deliberately setting aside time and place to come together enables us to live our testimonies more wholly when we are

Spiritual Nurture of Children within the Meeting Community

apart. We discover anew each year the creative tension between freedom for each child (and the child in each person) to explore their own spirituality and the desire to pass on the gifts we find in our Quaker culture. Whether we come from large urban meeting communities or small isolated worship groups, we need the sharing of ideas, the model of positive parenting, and the shelter of this community where the whole person and the whole family are included. We know it is sustaining for all ages to encounter both struggles and successes within this caring community.

> *Young people raised among Quakers become Quakers....*
> *[if] they get hooked on the experience of a spiritual community; they become passionate about the truths learned by plunging into the living water together.*
> —Gail Eastwood, 2007. (3)

Queries

For individuals and families:

1. How do I/we get to know those of all ages within your meeting?
2. How do I/we receive spiritual nurture from younger meeting members?
3. How are regular worship times offered within my/our home, other than the weekly worship with the meeting?
4. How will my/our children learn about Spirit guiding actions within their home?
5. How does our family support others who have leadings?
6. How does our family share celebration of new life? Loss of a loved one? Face hard decisions such as a move?
7. How do we clearly express our beliefs and values to one another and to our children?
8. How do we include our children in our times of doubt, division, vulnerability and struggle?

FAITH AND PRACTICE

For meetings:

1. How do we open connection to beauty, mystery, and the Divine with our children?
2. How do we provide welcome during our meeting for worship for our infants and children?
3. How do we nurture and support faith-based actions of our youth and families outside the walls of the meetinghouse?
4. How do we work and play with young and older together within our meetings?
5. How do we support families in nurturing the spiritual growth of children?
6. How do we nurture in our children an understanding of the Divine and an understanding of the process of listening to the Spirit as they grow?
7. How do our children know who we are and what we stand for?
8. How do we create trusting, intentional welcoming environments to draw our youth into worship with us?
9. How does the meeting support young people as they move toward adulthood?
10. How does the meeting involve young people in committees and other service experiences?
11. How can our meeting actively name and nurture the spiritual gifts of each and every child that comes among us?

References:

1. Rufus Jones, *The Luminous Trail*, 1947, pp. 153–165, as quoted in *Rufus Jones Speaks to Our Time*, ed. Harry Emerson Fosdick (New York: The Macmillan Company, 1961), p. 240.
2. Based on comments from Northern Yearly Meeting teens during conversations at Madison Monthly Meeting, 2009.

3. Gail Eastwood, "It Takes a Meeting to Raise a Quaker," *Friends Journal*, July 2007.

Approved 2011

FAITH AND PRACTICE

Education

It is not too much to say that the two most important duties of our Society are to publish truth as we understand it and to educate our children in our faith and life.
—London Yearly Meeting, Friends Education Council, 1949. (1)

The belief that there is "that of God in each person" is the foundation of the Quaker approach to education. Education cultivates the fullness of the human spirit through both openness and discipline. We are open to the knowledge, understanding, and wisdom that come from history, from our own life experience of God, and from the works and lives of others. We recognize all of life as an educational enterprise that we are all teachers as well as learners.

Explicitly, spiritual education is centered on the family, the meeting, and the broader community of Friends. Institutional forms of education play an important role in most peoples' lives and these can also have a spiritual component that influences the character of an individual. Young people and their families are encouraged to pursue the educational path they are drawn to, whether it be public schools, Friends schools, independent schools, home schools, or in some other setting.

Friends have valued education since the Society's founding in the mid-17th century. Education, both spiritual and intellectual, was recognized as enabling an individual to better discern and communicate the promptings of the Spirit. As early as the 1660s, George Fox encouraged the establishment of boys' and girls' schools among the new Friends communities at Waltham and Shacklewell. Friends, with the encouragement of William Penn, opened schools in Pennsylvania in 1683. In 1689 Friends opened the Friends Public School in Philadelphia, which was open to all children long before universal public education. Friends saw education as an aid in their search for truth "...that so, from the oldest to the youngest truth may flow in its beauty and comeliness to God's glory and all His people's comfort." (2)

Friends' openness to continuing revelation leads us to place equal emphasis on the educational process, personal development, and educational content. Scripture and existing knowledge are important. People are led to think critically and take joy in discovering new implications of knowledge gained.

Quakers usually provide education for children, youth, and adults within the Meeting community. Monthly meetings are encouraged to provide both education for youth in First Day School and education for adults. Our education also takes place in our homes, in our schools, in our home schools and in the wider community.

Within the meeting community, meeting for worship and meeting for worship with attention to business provide valuable educational opportunities. Service to Northern Yearly Meeting and local meetings, such as committee work, also provides an opportunity to learn and grow.

With regard to Friends educational institutions within Northern Yearly Meeting, there is currently one kindergarten through eighth grade Friends school (Friends School of Minnesota in St. Paul) and Camp Woodbrooke, a youth and family camp in Richland Center, Wisconsin. Scattergood Friends School, a grade nine through twelve boarding school, is located within Iowa Yearly Meeting (Conservative) and has attracted many Northern Year-

Education

ly Meeting families. In addition, Northern Yearly Meeting includes individuals who have attended and taught in other Friends schools, colleges, and study centers throughout the world. Northern Yearly Meeting also recognizes the benefits of home schooling; for families wishing to home school, the spiritual and nurturing resources of the yearly meeting may be used to support this effort.

Northern Yearly Meeting and its constituent meetings provide many educational opportunities through speakers, workshops, meeting libraries, interest groups, regional gatherings, Northern Yearly Meeting annual sessions, First Day School, couple enrichment, and Spiritual Nurture programs. Friends For a Nonviolent World (FNVW), the Saint Paul-based peace organization, provides valuable programs and activities.

Friends' educational opportunities outside of Northern Yearly Meeting are abundant. Because Quaker faith encourages witness through action, there exist Friends organizations such as Friends Committee on National Legislation (FCNL), American Friends Service Committee (AFSC), and Right Sharing of World Resources (RSWR) serve to help us understand the relationship between faith and action while actively working to bring about positive social change. Friends General Conference is an important educational resource, as are Quaker study centers such as Pendle Hill.

We recognize that supporting these various educational paths is important for the Friends community and for the common good of the wider community. To this end, we unite with Philadelphia Yearly Meeting's Covenant on Education, which calls "on all families, meetings, and schools...to support and embrace the following goals":

> • *To encourage our local public schools and teachers and parents in their efforts to provide an education of great value to the children of our communities, through participation as teachers, members of school boards, advisory councils,*

advocacy groups, as volunteers, and as advocates for public funding for education.
* *To affirm our commitment to our Friends schools and their spiritual basis through service as teachers, school committee members, parents and students.*
* *To support Friends who work in Quaker education, and to create a climate that encourages Friends to go into teaching in Friends schools.*

As Friends, we should work to strengthen both Friends schools and public education because through both of them we strengthen our community and society. (3)

As teachers and parents, we need to be mindful of how our actions speak. When we proclaim ourselves as Friends of the Truth we acknowledge our responsibility as models for others.

Queries

For individuals:

1. In what ways do I share my deepest experiences, struggles, concerns and beliefs with children and others?
2. Do I devote sufficient attention to developing my own understanding of the history and practices of the Religious Society of Friends?
3. What educational opportunities do I pursue that enhance my spiritual growth?
4. In what ways do I feel led to take responsibility for supporting others' education?

For meetings:

1. How does our meeting provide for educating children and adults within its community?
2. How does our meeting attend to educating its members and

Education

attenders about the history and practices of the Religious Society of Friends?
3. How does our meeting encourage people to develop their potential as the Spirit leads them?
4. How does our meeting support education, in terms of Friends schools, home schools and public education?

References:

1. London Yearly Meeting, *Friends Education Council: Up to Eighteen*, 1949, p. 7.
2. Bristol Yearly Meeting, 1695, as quoted in *Quaker Faith and Practice*, London Yearly Meeting, 1994, 23.72.
3. Philadelphia Yearly Meeting, *Covenant on Education*, approved July, 1999. http://www.pym.org/friends-and-education/covenant-on-education/ (accessed 5 September 2016).

Approved 2005

Faith and Practice

Preparing for Death

Death, then, being the Way and Condition of life, we cannot love to live, if we cannot bear to die...Death is but crossing the world, as friends do the seas; they live in one another still...
—William Penn, 1693. (1)

*God calls our loved ones, but we lose not wholly
What He hath given;
They live on earth, in thought and deed, as truly
As in His heaven.*
—John Greenleaf Whittier, 1857. (2)

Friends, like all people, live with issues of death and dying. Early Friends faced somewhat different death issues than do Friends today. For early Friends, infant mortality was high. For example, only two of William Penn's seven children by his first wife survived into adulthood. The average life expectancy at birth was less and death often came at a young age, from infection or trauma, usually at home, and sometimes in prison (the last epidemic of bubonic plague in London was in 1665–6).

Today, life expectancy in the United States is in the 70s and 80s, with many living longer. We face an aging population with the attendant problems of caring for disabilities and loss of independent living capabilities. New medical technologies keep people alive for prolonged periods, at times in persistent vegetative states. People die in hospitals as well as in homes. Hospice care is often available.

Doctor-assisted suicide and euthanasia are issues not addressed before modern times. Friends today have not reached agreement on these issues: historical testimonies on the sanctity of human life, the importance of the quality of life, and personal decision-making may present conflicts when considering issues of euthanasia and assisted suicide.

Death is a natural occurrence. We will all die and sometimes death may be welcomed. Meetings and their members and attenders have responsibilities to each other and to society in decisions surrounding death.

Meeting Responsibilities

All meetings and worship groups are encouraged to:

- regularly discuss the making of decisions about death and disability
- encourage individual members to give prayer and thought to these issues and provide informed advice and counsel to Friends and attenders
- consider providing, and keeping on file forms that record individual information and wishes.

Larger meetings often have a memorial committee or a committee of care to assist when death is anticipated and when it occurs. In some meetings the Committee on Oversight or Ministry and Counsel handles these matters. Small meetings may have more difficulty than larger meetings doing these tasks but could consider asking larger meetings for help. Meetings can collect and provide information about 1) hospice care, 2) funeral homes, 3) memorial societies and funeral consumer alliances that assist in simple and less expensive funerals and burials, 4) home funerals,

Preparing for Death

5) green burials, and 6) legal requirements at the time of death. This can be a great gift and provide helpful guidance.

Emotional Support: The meeting can pray for those involved and provide emotional support by being present when needed and by helping with other care. Friends are encouraged to show sympathy to those grieving with phone calls, cards, and visits, being careful that their actions are not burdensome or intrusive. Need for support may be long-term, since grief may be a cyclical process and re-emerge months after the death of a loved one – particularly at times when the loss may be felt more keenly such as at holidays and the first anniversary of the death.

Coordination of Care: Meetings can coordinate care for a member who is dying by arranging for meals and child care if needed. Personal care services, and other practical aid both before and after death, both to the dying person and to family members, may be helpful. The meeting or a committee can coordinate phone calls, help with the funeral and memorial service arrangements, help write and arrange for publication of the obituary in consultation with the family, and notify insurance companies.

Memorial Meeting for Worship: Monthly meetings, in consultation with family and/or caregivers, may plan to celebrate the life of a departed Friend in a loving manner. This may take the form of a called meeting for worship. During this worship Friends recognize the universal experience of death and give emotional support to the loved ones. This called meeting for worship can be either programmed or unprogrammed. The clerk of the meeting or a designee explains the format for the service, especially for those present who might not be familiar with Quaker worship. If the memorial service is programmed, designated individuals may give tributes to the departed person. The worship may include reading favorite Bible passages, Quaker writings, or poetry, singing favorite songs, or playing favorite music of the individual, the individual's loved ones or family. The family often participates. Open grieving is appropriate in this worship.

Memorial Minutes: Monthly Meetings may prepare a memorial minute to forward to the Yearly Meeting for the annual session. Information that the departed person may have provided would be helpful in preparing this minute.

Clearness Committee: At times a clearness committee for a dying person may be appropriate to meet with the person, provide spiritual support, discuss issues of reconciliation and forgiveness if such issues exist, and give the dying person an opportunity to share concerns about the dying process. This clearness committee might also assist in a called meeting for worship (a living memorial worship) should one be requested by the dying person. This could provide a joyful opportunity to celebrate a life.

Personal and Family Responsibilities

Friends have individual responsibilities for themselves and for each other in decisions surrounding death. Friends' testimony on simplicity should be considered in making decisions about death. Each person is urged to give thoughtful consideration to the following:

A **legal will** provides for distribution of belongings and one's estate. This is sound stewardship, helps prevent dispute among family members, and may give comfort to those surviving. Friends could consider the opportunity to make significant gifts to Quaker and other charitable organizations. Current tax laws regarding estate taxes, trusts, and gifts of appreciated stock when taken into account may be beneficial to both the donor, the heirs, and recipient organizations. A will also provides parents the opportunity to designate guardians for their dependent children.

A **living will** provides a medical directive, a durable power of attorney for health care, and similar documents that can provide guidance for others about the individual's wishes. These may be separate documents or one document may cover them all. The form and requirements vary from state to state. Medical clinics, hospitals, and doctors offices have the forms and information. Before becoming unable to participate in decision-making, individuals may consider sharing their desires for care with family, friends, and physician(s). This is different from a legal will, which is for disposition of property.

Disability and Long-Term Care: The aging process can be accompanied by decreased physical and/or mental ability. Often these conditions create situations where neither family nor friends can completely meet the needs that are present. With an aging population more people are in nursing homes. Thus individuals may want to consider arrangements for long-term care if disability occurs. Keeping apprised of alternative care options may include investing in personal long-term care insurance and investigating assisted living options or nursing home care. Friends can assist in making these life decisions.

Organ Donation: Instructions can be made for donations of organs or the body. Many states have provisions on driver's licenses for organ donations that may give new hope for life to others. The nearest medical school has forms for body donations for medical education.

Body Disposition: Unless donated to a medical school, wishes for disposition of the body by burial or cremation may be a helpful guide to survivors, even though these wishes may not be legally binding. Options for simple, inexpensive burials are available.

Memorial Meeting: Stating elements to include in a memorial meeting for worship such as favorite Scripture passages, songs, poems, or other readings is helpful to those planning this event.

Obituary and Other Information: Preparing a written obituary is another helpful act for loved ones left behind. These notes may be given to the newspaper and used in the memorial worship or in a memorial minute. Other useful information for families would be a list of persons and organizations to be notified in the event of death. Some of this information should be shared with loved ones, other important persons, appropriate meeting members, the executor of your estate and others. The information should be readily available—not just placed in a safety deposit box where it may not be accessible upon death.

While this chapter is about death and dying, Friends are reminded of the importance of celebrating significant milestones (birthdays, anniversaries, etc.) with family, friends, and the faith community.

Resources

Aging with Dignity, P.O. Box 1661, Tallahassee, FL 32302-1661. The organization provides a form titled "Five Wishes." 1-888-5WISHES (1-888-594-7437) https://agingwithdignity.org/

Funeral Consumers Alliance, a national umbrella connected with over 100 local nonprofit groups which offer consumer information and reduced prices on funeral services for members (one-time membership rates are very reasonable). https://www.funerals.org/

Morgan, Ernest, *Dealing Creatively with Death: A Manual of Death Education and Simple Burial*, 13th ed. (Bayside, New York: Barclay House, 1994), 163 pp.

Preparing for Death

Queries

For individuals:

1. What thought have I given towards preparation for my death?
2. How have I expressed my wishes should I die or become incapacitated; how have I informed my family, meeting, and executor?

For meetings:

1. How has our monthly meeting addressed issues of death and dying?
2. In what way has our monthly meeting prepared to carry out its responsibilities in the event of a death in the meeting?
3. What vehicle does our monthly meeting have for recording individual's wishes?

References:

1. William Penn, *Some Fruits of Solitude,* 1693. Republished by Friends United Press 1st ed. May, 1978, p. 71 (#505). Also quoted in *Quaker Faith and Practice* of Britain Yearly Meeting,1995; 22:95.
2. John Greenleaf Whittier, "To my Friend on the Death of his Sister," *The Poetical Works of Whittier* (Boston: Houghton Mifflin Company, , 1894), p. 46. First published by Whittier in 1857.

Approved 2001, information added 2016

Faith and Practice

HISTORY

...part of the vocation of a prophetic people is to see their present struggles in the perspective of their larger history....Each new phase of Quaker history has been an attempt to rebalance the shifting energies of our faith and practice, while discovering new horizons of mission and service in the world.

>Douglas Gwyn, *A Sustainable Life*, Quaker Press of FGC, 2014, pp. 96 and 108.

A Brief History of Quakerism

The Religious Society of Friends arose in seventeenth-century England at a time when Bible translations in English were becoming less expensive and more available to non-clergy. It was a time of great religious and political turmoil. There was great dissatisfaction with the established Church of England, with its legal monopoly of public worship, oppressive tithes, and corruption. Dissenting groups, including Roman Catholics, Presbyterians, Puritans, Ranters, and Muggletonians vied for the spiritual and political loyalties of the populace, and in the case of the first two, for control of the government. During this time of civil war, Oliver Cromwell, the leader of the puritanical revolutionaries called "roundheads," held the title of Protector and was the head of the government.

As a young man, George Fox, a leather worker, walked throughout England seeking someone who could guide him to authentic religious experience. He was exposed to many of the theological ideas and practices of the time, but found no satisfaction until a day in 1647 when he had a profound religious experience, which he recorded in his *Journal*:

> And when all my hopes in...all men were gone, so that I had nothing outwardly to help me, nor could tell what to do, then, Oh then, I heard a voice which said "There is

FAITH AND PRACTICE

*one, even Christ Jesus, that can speak to thy condition,"
and when I heard it my heart did leap for joy.*
—George Fox, 1647. (1)

Thereafter, Fox became the leader of a loosely-knit group of traveling evangelists, some of whom were already convinced of the same truths Fox was preaching, and some of whom were convinced by him or others. The founding date of Quakerism is generally given as 1652. Fox climbed a large rock ridge in northwest England, called Pendle Hill, and looking westward toward the sea he had a vision of a great people to be gathered. Soon thereafter he preached to a large gathering at Firbank Fell and started a wave of conversions. About half of the early Quaker leaders came from this event.

One of his early converts was Margaret Fell. Small groups of seekers in the northwest of England, and later throughout the rest of the country, responded to the fervent message of George Fox and Margaret Fell. Margaret Fell was the wife of a judge, mother of a large family, and manager of a large estate. While her husband, Judge Fell was riding the circuit, the Fell home became the home office of the new movement, with Margaret Fell doing much of the needed work, corresponding with the traveling ministers, and bailing them out when they were arrested. She and her daughters also cared for them and nursed them back to health after periods of imprisonment. Judge Fell was supportive and protective but could not join the movement without sacrificing his position. After Judge Fell's death, George Fox and Margaret Fell were married.

Margaret Fell clearly contributed to the practice of equality of women in Quakerism. She wrote a pamphlet advocating the right of women to speak in public. At a time when women had no rights, Quakers were unique among the faith groups that survived this period in professing and widely practicing equality of the genders.

A Brief History of Quakerism

Fox's distinctive message was that God was equally available to all people, without the mediation of priest, Bible, creed, consecrated building, or outward sacraments. This belief led to the holding of meetings for worship in any convenient place, based in silence with all free to minister. Friends refused to pay tithes and followed such provocative practices as contradicting priests in their own churches, refusing to remove their hats in deference to officers of government, addressing all by the familiar terms of "thee" and "thou" rather than the deferential "you" and refusing to take oaths.

Friends were persecuted by governments of all shades because of their aggressive insistence on these and other "heretical" and "unreasonable" practices. Many lost all their property. It is estimated that of 50,000 Friends in England, ten percent were imprisoned between 1660 and 1689, and many died as a result. In America, four Friends were hanged in Boston Common by the government of the Massachusetts Colony.

One young convert was William Penn, son of the Admiral of the same name. Trained in law and theology, both profoundly spiritual and sufficiently worldly with useful aristocratic connections, Penn rose rapidly to a position of leadership after he became a Friend. He wrote well and extensively and defended himself in a trial, which established the independent power of the jury in English law. He was given land in the New World in settlement of a debt owed by the King to his father, Admiral Penn. The King named this land Pennsylvania, in honor of Admiral Penn. Pennsylvania became a haven for religious refugees from Britain and the Continent and contributed to the ultimate establishment of religious freedom in the United States.

Period of Quietism

The close of the seventeenth century brought an end to persecutions. Friends were strongly established in Britain and North

America, and were the dominant religious group in many colonies in addition to Pennsylvania. By then, a structure of meetings, from local to the national Yearly Meeting, had been established in Britain with several yearly meetings in the colonies, which George Fox had visited.

The testimonies of integrity, peace, equality, and simplicity were clarified and began to harden into rigid rules for which members could not only be "eldered," but also "read out of meeting." The period of quietism had begun, and lasted through the eighteenth century. The plain clothes and plain speech, which had been powerful revolutionary symbols of equality and simplicity, lingered on to be the peculiar ways of a peculiar people.

Deviation from the prescribed norms became the basis for admonition and even "disownment." One cause of disownment was "marrying out" to someone not a Friend. Naturally, this caused a decline in membership. Patterns of organization and membership, originally developed as protections against persecution, became straitjackets to protect against contamination by the world. Schools were established to provide "guarded education."

For those who were comfortable within the fold, this period of quietism provided an exemplary way of life, of loving communities characterized by simplicity and serenity. A fine example of this way of life was John Woolman (1720–1772) of Mount Holly, New Jersey. Growing up in a sheltering family and meeting, he learned tailoring and shop keeping as adjuncts to a deep spiritual life. When he found himself in danger of becoming a prosperous merchant, he cut back his activities to tailoring and his small farm so that he would not be "cumbered" by possessions and would have time to follow the leadings of the spirit.

As a young clerk in a shop, he was asked to write a bill of sale for a slave. This traumatic experience led him to his life calling from God. He traveled by foot and horseback up and down the colonies, persuading Quaker slave owners to free their slaves. He also worked in the business sessions of Philadelphia Yearly Meeting to obtain the adoption of minutes against slave holding. As a result, primarily of the efforts of John Woolman and others, most American Quakers had given up slave holding by the time of the Revolutionary War. Woolman's *Journal* is a classic not only of Quakerism but also of American literature.

Friends were, with few exceptions, neutral in the French and Indian and Revolutionary Wars; this cost them a great deal in membership and influence. This loss was compounded by a serious schism early in the nineteenth century.

The Great Separation

During the period of quietism, British Friends in general had become converted to an evangelical Christianity that accepted orthodox Christian theological dogmas in an almost creedal form. This movement spread to America at about the same time as a general growth of deism. Deists generally believed in a creator who did not intervene thereafter, and they were skeptical of the historic authenticity of the Bible. Many of the revolutionary "founding fathers" were Deists. American Friends tended to drift in both directions, leading to serious conflicts over theological issues. British Friends came over to America to support "true" orthodoxy against those Friends who argued that the "Inner Light" was to be honored above the Bible and traditional Christian doctrines.

Prominent among the latter was Elias Hicks, a Long Island farmer and minister, who was widely popular as a preacher, not only to Friends but also to the general religious public. Hicks was a powerful speaker, emphasizing the primacy of guidance by the Light Within over all other religious authorities. Hicks became the principal target of the British evangelicals, some of whom followed him from meeting to meeting in an effort to overcome his influence.

The conflict came to a head in Philadelphia Yearly Meeting in

1827, where urban wealth was allied with Christian orthodoxy and rural simplicity was allied with the message of Hicks. The sessions ended with two Philadelphia Yearly Meetings, one Orthodox and the other Hicksite. The split moved on to New York, Canada, Baltimore, and the newly established Ohio Yearly Meeting. In New England and the Carolinas, Hicksite Friends were not numerous enough to establish separate yearly meetings. All the new yearly meetings in the Middle West and Canada were related to one or the other camp.

Quakers were a part of the westward movement of European settlement across the continent. As Orthodox Friends continued to be influenced by evangelical movements in other protestant groups, they adopted many of the practices of these churches, including the use of organs, programmed worship services, paid ministers, steeples on their churches, and missionaries. This also occurred in the eastern Orthodox yearly meetings in America, except for Philadelphia. In New England Yearly Meeting, this produced another split in 1854. John Wilbur, a Rhode Island schoolteacher, objected to these changes and took his case to the Yearly Meeting sessions. The resultant split produced a small yearly meeting (Wilburite) and a much larger one, called Gurneyite for Joseph John Gurney, the most prominent British Evangelical Friend. Today's Conservative Meetings in Ohio, Iowa, and North Carolina originated from the Wilburite split.

Nineteenth-century Developments

To avoid living in a slave culture, many Friends moved from the south to the Northwest Territory (which became the states of Ohio, Indiana, Illinois, Michigan, and Wisconsin). Established by the Ordinance of 1787, it was to be "forever free" of slavery. For example, large numbers left the Carolinas for Indiana. Substantial numbers later moved on to Iowa, Kansas, Nebraska, California, and Oregon. Toward the end of the century, the Gurneyite movement split again, with the most evangelical yearly meetings separating from the main body of Orthodox, who had become more to resemble mainstream protestant denominations. These evangelical yearly meetings now constitute the Evangelical Friends Church International.

Friends of all persuasions were active against slavery, founding antislavery societies, editing abolitionist papers, and playing an important role in supporting the escaped slave leaders of the "underground railroad" to help more slaves escape across the free but perilous northern states to Canada. Quaker women, first active in the anti-slavery movement, became the dominant leadership of nineteenth-century movements for women's rights. Especially notable were Lucretia Coffin Mott and the Grimke sisters.

Friends also continued to struggle for fair treatment of Native Americans, to the extent that President Grant appointed a Quaker as Commissioner of Indian Affairs. Friends' efforts at fair treatment were overwhelmed by the land-hungry anti-Indian sentiment. This sentiment supported the illegal settlers who invaded the Indian lands.

Many Quakers served as agents on the newly demarcated Indian reservations and established schools for Native children. Believing that assimilation was the best option for Native people's survival, they required Native children to adopt European-American manners of dress, language, gender roles, and Christian teachings. Despite their good intentions, the forced assimilation policy did great harm to Native children and families. (2)

The Civil War was as traumatic for Friends as for the nation as a whole. Sympathies were sharply against slavery, but the peace testimony was strong. Some Friends enlisted and fought, but many Friends took advantage of the opportunity to "buy out" of the draft. In general, efforts at peacemaking were not well received.

Friends celebrated the Emancipation Proclamation as the end

to state-sanctioned slavery when it came. They also recognized that many formerly enslaved people continued to face enormous structural barriers and challenges to survival and success. Quakers joined with many other denominations to provide schools for formerly enslaved adults and children. These schools provided critically important educational opportunities and continued to reinforce segregation practices in both the North and South. (3)

Toward the end of the nineteenth century, vigorous leadership in all branches revived Quakerism, which had hardened both North American and British Friends into virtual denial of one another's existence. Hicksite and Orthodox Friends would not accept one another's communications, and London Yearly Meeting refused to be in correspondence with the Hicksites. Even yearly meetings that agreed in theology, form of worship, and structure had little to do with one another except in the exchange of formal epistles—letters "to Friends Everywhere"—drafted by yearly meeting sessions.

George Fox had encouraged the setting up of Friends schools, as did William Penn. These efforts had developed by the end of the nineteenth century into a network of secondary boarding schools in Britain and the eastern United States and high schools in Washington, New York City, Baltimore, and Philadelphia. These were followed by colleges established in Pennsylvania, North Carolina, Ohio, Indiana, Iowa, Kansas, California, and Oregon.

Twentieth-century Movements

The harsh separateness of Friends in the nineteenth century was changed through the leadership of a remarkable group of young men on both sides of the Atlantic. The principal figure in North America was Rufus Jones, born in 1863 in the small Quaker village of South China, Maine, which was in the Gurneyite New England Yearly Meeting. He was educated in Quaker schools and Haverford College, with graduate study at Harvard. He had a long teaching career at Haverford. His central academic interests were in Quaker history, mysticism, and devotion. Jones was also involved in church affairs, and while quite young became the editor of the *American Friend*, the principal journal of Gurneyite Quakerism. He also was involved in the process that led to the organization of the Friends Five Years Meeting, (now Friends United Meeting), an association of Gurneyite yearly meetings formed in 1900. Jones was not a supporter of the Richmond Declaration of Faith, a strong statement of Christian orthodoxy prepared at a large conference in 1887, and was influential in preventing it from becoming the basis of association of the Five Years Meeting.

At this same time, about 1900, a group of Hicksite leaders brought their yearly meetings together in the Friends General Conference (FGC). These two groups, though reconciled to one another, were the beginnings of a movement for unity that brought all Friends closer together in the next century.

In response to the harsh treatment of conscientious objectors in the World War of 1914–1918, the American Friends Service Committee (AFSC) was organized in 1917 to provide alternative service. Although located in Philadelphia, it was supported by Friends from many yearly meetings and was established as an independent corporation. Rufus Jones served as Clerk of the Board. The AFSC has followed the Quaker tradition of relief work, feeding children on both sides of the Spanish Civil War and in Germany after both world wars. It has since grown into a very influential peace and justice organization, supported by many Friends, as well as by many who are not Friends. In 1947 The Religious Society of Friends received the Nobel Peace Prize for its humanitarian work; the AFSC and its counterpart in Britain accepted the award.

At the end of World War II, the Friends' Committee on National Legislation (FCNL) evolved from the AFSC to be the Quaker lobby in Washington. FCNL has been, and is, of great value to Friends concerned with right governmental action. It is supported by many U.S. yearly meetings and is recognized as one of the most accurate and reliable sources of Washington information.

In education, the twentieth century brought residential adult study centers in Birmingham, England, and suburban Philadelphia, summer camps for children, several yearly meeting retreat centers, and a new college in New York. Of great importance also was the founding in 1960 of the Earlham School of Religion at Earlham College in Richmond, Indiana. It was designed to provide pastors for Friends United Meeting (FUM) churches with high quality training and a strong background in Quakerism. It has also provided the same opportunity for many Friends of other backgrounds.

Other forms of closer association have developed over the years. In 1931, Fifty-seventh Street Meeting was established in Chicago, belonging to both Illinois Yearly Meeting (FGC) and Western Yearly Meeting (FUM). Then, in the 1940s and 1950s, several yearly meetings that had split in 1827 but soon after were reunited: Philadelphia, Canadian, New England, New York, and Baltimore. All these belong to FGC and all but Philadelphia also belong to FUM.

During this time, Rufus Jones continued to be the most prominent Quaker in the U.S., speaking widely among Friends, lecturing on the prestigious ecumenical religious lecture circuit, writing constantly (history of Quakerism, mysticism, devotions), promoting unity among Friends, and teaching at Haverford College. His assertion that Quakerism was essentially a mystical religion brought him more into favor with Hicksite Friends and less with Orthodox Friends, despite his Orthodox roots and long affiliation with Haverford, which was founded by Philadelphia Orthodox Friends. In a way this made him a bridge and furthered unity, since many Orthodox Friends continued to admire him.

In the middle of the century, there was new growth of Hicksite and other "liberal" Quaker groups in the U.S. For example, in

A Brief History of Quakerism

1938 there were only two functioning monthly meetings in Illinois Yearly Meeting (FGC)–Fifty-Seventh Street in the University of Chicago neighborhood, and Clear Creek, which met in the Illinois Yearly Meetinghouse at McNabb. In the following fifty years there came to be a meeting or worship group in many university and college communities in Illinois, Missouri, Wisconsin, and Minnesota. This provided the strength in numbers to make possible the organization of Northern Yearly Meeting as a separate body. A comparable growth occurred on the West Coast. Pacific Yearly Meeting, Hicksite in spirit though not affiliated with Friends General Conference, divided to add North Pacific and Intermountain Yearly Meetings. There has also been a substantial growth in the former California Yearly Meeting (FUM), which is now Southwest Yearly Meeting in the Evangelical Friends Church International (EFCI). This expansion in the Middle West and west occurred during a period of decline in numbers of Friends in Britain and the eastern United States.

FWCC (Friends World Committee for Consultation) works at the world level, connecting Friends, crossing cultures, and changing lives. It functions in consultation, not favoring a particular agenda among world Quakers. Working both vertically and horizontally FWCC represents Friends at the world level.

In 1920 the first World Conference of Friends was held in London. A second conference in 1937 at Swarthmore College in Pennsylvania resulted in the creation of the Friends World Committee for Consultation, which has grown in membership to include a majority of yearly meetings in the world. As its name suggests, it has no authority over its members, but is a catalyst for Friends meeting together to share their spiritual lives, challenges and joys on a personal, human level. FWCC is organized into four sections: Africa, Asia-West Pacific, Europe and Middle East, and the Americas. These sections hold annual meetings to maintain spiritual contact and consider issues in their regions. FWCC uses its international character to qualify as the sponsor of the Quaker programs at the United Nations in New York and Geneva, and connects Friends to a wide variety of Quaker organization to foster growth and a better world.

The presence of Quakers arose in several locations through missionary work. This work was undertaken by Friends in Friends United Meeting and Evangelical Friends Church International yearly meetings. The yearly meetings established now thrive independently of mission work and work cooperatively with outside organizations. Some of the regions of strongest growth have been in East Africa, Central America, and the Andean highlands of Bolivia and Peru. As of the 2012 count of Quakers by FWCC, Kenya has the largest number of Friends in the world with 146, 300. Quakers in Bolivia and Peru number 25,800, with Central American countries of Guatemala, Honduras, Costa Rica, Nicaragua, and El Salvador home to 24,000 Friends. With 76,000 in the U.S., and 15,800 in Britain, and smaller numbers in other European and English-speaking countries, the majority of Quakers worldwide no longer live in North America and Britain. (4) Yearly meetings in the sections are providing spiritual and logistical leadership for world Quakerism with support from FWCC.

Another more recent development has been a renewal of the practice of traveling in the ministry. This practice, of inter-visitation by Friends of one meeting to other meetings, was important in the early knitting of The Religious Society of Friends and is recognized as one of the most important methods for promoting ties among Friends across geographical and organizational boundaries. Northern Yearly Meeting Friends are active in yearly meeting, national, and international programs of such travel.

References:

A primary source for the original version of this chapter was Hugh

A Brief History of Quakerism

Barbour and Jerry William Frost's *The Quakers*, published by Greenwood Publishing Group of Westport Connecticut in 1988.

1. *The Journal of George Fox*, revised edition by John L. Nickalls, Philadelphia Yearly Meeting, 1997, p. 11.
2. For more information, see the National Native American Boarding School Healing Coalition http://www.boardingschoolhealing.org/ (accessed 20 August 2016) and Boulder Friends Meeting Research on Quaker Indian Day Schools and Boarding Schools http://www.boulderfriendsmeeting.org/ipc-boarding-school-research/ (accessed 20 August 2016)
3. For a thorough treatment of Friends' evolving views and practices in regard to racial justice and inclusion, see *Fit for Freedom, Not for Friendship: Quakers, African Americans and the Myth of Racial Justice*, by Vanessa Julye and Donna McDaniel, Quaker Press, 2009.
4. "Finding Quakers Around the World," Friends World Committee for Consultation, 2012. Downloaded from http://fwccamericas.org/Map.shtml (accessed 5 September 2016).

Approved 2005, Revised 2016

Faith and Practice

A Brief History of the Peace Testimony

From Early Quakers to Contemporary Friends

The Roots of Our Peace Witness

The classic, oft-quoted statement of the Quaker Peace Testimony is the Declaration to King Charles II of 1660 signed by twelve Friends including George Fox, one of the founders of the Religious Society of Friends. The Declaration is about four and one half pages long with only part of it quoted here, as is the custom. This was sent to reassure the King that Quakers were a peaceful people and should not be grouped with those trying to overthrow the King. The Declaration starts with: "A Declaration from the harmless and innocent people of God, called Quakers,..."

> *Our principle is, and our practices have always been, to seek peace and ensue it and to follow after righteousness and the knowledge of God, seeking the good and welfare and doing that which tends to the peace of all...All bloody principles and practices, we, as to our own particulars, do utterly deny, with all outward wars and strife and fightings with outward weapons, for any end or under any pretence whatsoever. And this is our testimony to the whole world.*

> ...That the spirit of Christ, by which we are guided, is not changeable, so as once to command us from a thing as evil and again to move unto it; and we do certainly know, and so testify to the world, that the spirit of Christ, which leads us into all Truth, will never move us to fight and war against any man with outward weapons, neither for the kingdom of Christ, nor for the kingdoms of this world.
>
> ...And as for the kingdoms of this world, we cannot covet them, much less can we fight for them...and that they may all come to witness the prophet's words who said, "Nation shall not lift up sword against nation, neither shall they learn war any more."
> —Isa. ii. 4; Mic. iv. 3. (1)

George Fox was imprisoned in 1651 for blasphemy. He was offered a commission in the militia, which if accepted would have freed him. He refused. Another frequently quoted statement is his refusal, as recorded in his journal:

> But I told them [the Commonwealth Commissioners] I lived in the virtue of that life and power that took away the occasion of all wars, and I knew from whence all wars did rise, from the lust according to James's doctrine. (James, iv. 1.)...I told them I was come into the covenant of peace which was before wars and strife were. (2)

A less well known statement and less often quoted is that of Margaret Fell, delivered to King Charles II in June of 1660, and intended for the King and both houses of Parliament:

> We are a people that follow after those things that make for peace, love and unity; it is our desire that others' feet may walk in the same, and do deny and bear our testimony against all strife, and wars, and contentions that

come from the lusts that war in the members, that war in the soul, which we wait for, and watch for in all people, and love and desire the good of all. (3)

John Woolman, best known for his work against slavery in this country in the mid to late 18th Century, raises in his "A Plea for the Poor" another aspect of war:

May we look upon our treasures, and the furniture of our houses and the garments in which we array ourselves and try whether the seeds of war have any nourishment in these our possessions or not. (4)

A Brief History of Our Peace Witness

Although Quakers are known for our peace testimony, it has not been an easy witness to adhere to. Individual Quakers throughout our history have displayed a wide range of responses to armed struggle.

Fox was clear that for him, personally, he could not participate in war. In some of his other writings, however, he accepted the authority of the state to use the sword. (5)

With war pending, in 1675, five Quakers in Rhode Island courageously approached the Wampanoag Indian tribal chief, unarmed, attempting to mediate a peace agreement to prevent what became known as King Phillip's War. They failed. When war broke out the death toll was frightful. The Quaker dominated administration and legislature in Rhode Island joined the war. Those who refused to fight were accused of complicity in the death of white settlers. (6)

Based on the trust William Penn developed with the Delaware Lenape Indians and the treaty, apparently oral, early Pennsylvania Quakers lived in peace with the Lenape for 70–75 years while war raged around them. The trust was gradually broken by the taking of Indian land by white settlers culminating with the

"Walking Purchase" of 1737 that violated the spirit of agreement Penn had made. The peace completely ended with the outbreak of the French and Indian War in 1756. (7)

Many Quakers declared that they would not participate in the rebellion against King George (the Revolutionary War) and as a result had to find a replacement to fight for them. Otherwise they were fined, or had property and goods confiscated; a few went to prison. Those that supported the war formed a separate group called the Free Quakers. (8)

In the Civil War, Quakers both fought in the war and were conscientious objectors vigorously opposing the war. (9)

In World War II an estimated 90% of eligible Quaker males in the U.S. joined the military on active duty as both combatants and noncombatants. Under the Selective Service Act of 1940 conscientious objection was an option and an estimated 12,000 men opted for this and served in Civilian Public Service Camps. (10)

In the Vietnam War, some joined the military but there was widespread protest by Quakers including draft resistance, war tax resistance, and other forms of civil disobedience. (11) One Friend set himself on fire in front of the Pentagon to call attention to the injustice of that war. (12)

Despite the range of individual response to war, the peace testimony remained a major public Friends testimony. Since 1774, London (now Britain) Yearly Meeting minuted its public testimony against war during both popular and unpopular wars. (13)

In 1987, Aotearoa/New Zealand Yearly Meeting made a strong public statement of the Quaker Peace Testimony to a committee of its government, which read in part:

We totally oppose all wars, all preparation for war, all use of weapons and coercion by force, and all military alliances; no end could ever justify such means.

We equally and actively oppose all that leads to violence

A Brief History of the Peace Testimony

among people and nations, and violence to other species and to our planet....

Refusal to fight with weapons is not surrender. We are not passive when threatened by the greedy, the cruel, the tyrant, the unjust.

We will struggle to remove the causes of impasse and confrontation by every means of nonviolent resistance available.

...We must start with our own hearts and minds...

The places to begin acquiring the skills and maturity and generosity to avoid or to resolve conflicts are in our own homes, our personal relationships, our schools, our workplaces, and wherever decisions are made. (14)

In the United States, Quaker groups reaffirmed the peace testimony after the two major world wars, again in 1960, which was the 300th anniversary of the Declaration, and again after the attack on the United States on September 11, 2001, and the subsequent U.S. wars. The most recent of these was a consultation sponsored by FWCC, which met at Guilford College in January 2003. (15)

The history of Friends and their practice of the Peace Testimony has continually changed, as the situations in the world demand different responses. Twentieth century Quakers had very specific issues during World War I, World War II, and the Cold War because of the nationwide military draft, and the need for all Quaker communities to help their young people respond. National Quaker leaders from various branches of Friends, who were separate theologically, nevertheless came together to help organize a way for young men to offer service rather than carry guns. This organization became the American Friends Service Committee in June of 1917.

FAITH AND PRACTICE

There was a similar service in Great Britain, the Friends Service Council. The world recognized the positive worth of these groups by awarding them the Nobel Peace Prize in 1947. The Nobel committee cited the role of all Quakers, "It is the silent help from the nameless to the nameless," in promoting the brotherhood among all nations, and used the AFSC and the Friends Service Council for this recognition. (16)

The history of our own yearly meeting began during World War II, when people who held peace concerns came together in a community. They were seeking spiritual nurture and support to sustain these peace concerns and to support their difficult work as conscientious objectors. Many local meetings formed and grew again during the years of our presence in Vietnam. We carry a passion to embody this testimony in our work, in our play, and in our care for the world. Northern Yearly Meeting supports our national Quaker leaders in AFSC, Friends Committee on National Legislation, and the Friends World Committee for Consultation, which sponsors our work at the United Nations. The primary evidence that the peace testimony is alive in Northern Yearly Meeting is the daily witness of ordinary people in all aspects of their careers and their connections in our communities.

Assembled in annual session May 28–31, 2004, Northern Yearly Meeting minuted the following:

> *We strive to live in a manner to take away the occasion of all war. We reaffirm our traditional opposition to war and violence as instruments of national policy. We feel great sadness for the tragic, brutal events in Iraq, Afghanistan and elsewhere being committed in our name. We especially grieve for the killing and torture, which we have inevitably brought on by the dehumanizing acts of war.*
>
> *As Quakers from the United States, we acknowledge*

our complicity in, and seek forgiveness for, these acts of our government. We will continue to stand and work for peace and justice. We will continue to support those who for conscience sake refuse to participate in the military. We support those who, for conscience sake, refuse to pay taxes for war. We support those who are involved in non-violent peacemaking. (17)

References:

1. *The Journal of George Fox,* Revised edition. By John L. Nickalls Philadelphia Yearly Meeting, 1997 1952 pp. 398-400. (The Declaration was dated 11/1660 using the old calendar and 1/1661 using the new calendar, which accounts for the different dates seen.)
2. Ibid., p. 65.
3. Britain Yearly Meeting, *Quaker Faith & Practice,* Third Edition. 1995. 19.46.
4. John Woolman, "A Plea for the Poor" in *The Journal and Major Essays of John Woolman.* Edited by Phillips P. Moulton, 1971. Richmond, Indiana: Friends United Press. p. 255.
5. H. L. Ingle, *First Among Friends* (New York: Oxford University Press, , 1994) pp. 192–195, and endnote p. 329 #18. Ingle states on p. 194 "He [Fox] did not deny, and never did deny, the right of a nation's rulers to wield weapons in the defense of a just cause. The problem was in defining such a cause." Also see: John Spears, "How would George Fox respond to terrorism?" *Friends Journal* , January, 2005. http://www.friendsjournal.org/2005002/ (accessed 20 June 2016)
6. G. Jonas, *On Doing Good: The Quaker Experiment* (New York: Charles Scribner's Sons, 1971), pp. 21–23; also: P.

Brock, *Pacifism in the United States* (Princeton, NJ: Princeton University Press, 1968), pp. 40–42.
7. Jonas, pp. 26–55.
8. Brock, pp. 183–211.
9. Ibid., pp. 713–779.
10. A. Smith, "The Renewal Movement: The Peace Testimony and Modern Quakerism," *Quaker History* 1996:85 (Fall issue). http://www.quaker.org/renewal.html (accessed 2 August 2016).
11. Quakers in the World, "Peace Witness and Relief Efforts During the Vietnam War," http://www.quakersintheworld.org/quakers-in-action/315 (accessed 20 June 2016).
12. Ann Morrison Welsh, *Fire of the Heart: Norman Morrison's Legacy in Viet Nam and at Home.* (Pendle Hill Pamphlet #381, 2005).
13. Britain Yearly Meeting, *Quaker Faith & Practice.* Fifth Edition, 2013, 24.05 through 24.09.
14. Aotearoa/New Zealand YM Peace Statement made by Yearly Meeting in 1987, http://quaker.org.nz/ym-peace-statement.
15. *Friends' Peace Witness in a Time of War.* The publication of the major addresses at this consultation by Friends World Committee for Consultation, Section of the Americas, 2005.
16. Elizabeth Gray Vining, *Friend of Life: The Biography of Rufus M. Jones* (Philadelphia: Lippincott, 1958), p. 306.
17. The Northern Yearly Meeting of the Religious Society of Friends (Quakers) assembled in annual session May 28-31, 2004, approved this minute.

Approved 2008

The Early History of Northern Yearly Meeting

Early Migration of Friends to the Upper Midwest

Early movements of Friends away from the south and the eastern seaboard to the Midwest in the mid-1800s established Quakerism in this region. Pioneer Friends moved into Illinois beginning in the 1830s. They established rural meetings that still had roots in Ohio and Indiana Yearly Meetings. Friends began settling in Iowa as early as 1835, and finally received permission to become a yearly meeting in 1863.

Pioneer Friends came to Wisconsin and Minnesota where they established several meetings and an academy. The first meetinghouse was built in Minneapolis in 1851; thus Minneapolis Friends were among the founding meetings of Iowa Yearly Meeting. By 1890 there were about a dozen meetings scattered through Wisconsin and Minnesota, in two quarterly meetings. A financial panic of 1893 started a depression that wiped out many new settlements, including Friends, so that by 1905 there were only two or three meetings remaining in Minnesota. Two meetings in Wisconsin that had become pastoral, Valton and Sturgeon Bay, still continue a relationship with Iowa Yearly Meeting (Friends United Meeting).

During the Great Revival movement of the 1870s and 80s, Iowa Yearly Meeting, among others, experienced internal separations of meetings, based on organizational and theological differences. One yearly meeting recognized more absolute authority of the Bible and gradually hired pastors. This body became Iowa Yearly Meeting (Friends United Meeting). The other retained the historical form of waiting silent worship, which recognized scripture as the source of confirming the personal inward discoveries of Divine Light. This body became Iowa Yearly Meeting (Conservative).

Illinois Yearly Meeting (ILYM), organized in 1875, was fortunate to avoid the theological struggles of its neighbors both east and west. It remained primarily a rural yearly meeting that supported unprogrammed worship until the 1930s. Gradually it grew to include meetings from several metropolitan areas including Chicago (1931), Milwaukee (1942), Madison (1945), and Twin Cities (1956). Illinois Yearly Meeting affiliated with Friends General Conference after that body was established in 1900.

1930–1947:
The Search for Peace Brings Friends Together

The contemporary Friends Meetings in Madison, Milwaukee, and the Twin Cities have their antecedents in the peace movement just prior to and during World War II. In each community, individuals came together to share their search for spiritual strength to resist the approaching war, the imminent military draft, and to support one another in conscientious objection. After 1941 the public popularity of the war brought pacifists even closer together in projects and witness. They helped one another face the choices: Civilian Public Service, prison, or accepting non-combatant status in the military. All hoped for support from those who stayed in the community.

After 17 years of informal association and worship groups, Madison Monthly Meeting of Friends was formally organized as an independent monthly meeting in 1937 through the Friends Fellowship Council, which is no longer in existence. Visits with

The Early History of Northern Yearly Meeting

Chicago Friends helped Madison Friends develop ties to Illinois Yearly Meeting. These ties led to membership in Fox Valley Quarter of Illinois Yearly Meeting in 1945. Until 1960, some Chicago area meetings belonged to the Fox Valley Quarter. Others affiliated with the Chicago Quarter of Western Yearly Meeting, a Five Years Meeting that later affiliated with Friends United Meeting. ("Western" refers to Indiana, not to the entire United States) Many Chicago meetings were united, with dual membership in both yearly meetings. Madison Meeting maintained such membership until the establishment of Northern Half-yearly Meeting in 1960.

In Milwaukee, informal Quaker worship began in 1937 at the home of a local woman whose son had exposure to Quakerism and Rufus Jones at Haverford College. This group was supported through relationships with Friends active in the American Friends Service Committee office in Chicago. In August 1941 a formal worship group began to meet regularly and correspond with Evanston Meeting (part of Illinois Yearly Meeting and Western Yearly Meeting). In 1942 it became a preparative meeting under the care of Evanston Meeting and moved to independent monthly meeting status in 1950 with ties to both Western and Illinois Yearly Meetings. As Milwaukee Friends became more active with Friends in Wisconsin and Minnesota, the tie with Western Yearly Meeting was dissolved (in the late 50s). Milwaukee Friends Meeting remained affiliated with both Illinois and Northern Yearly Meetings until 2007 when it left ILYM.

Macalester College in St. Paul and the University of Minnesota in Minneapolis were sites of informal Quaker style spiritual search groups as the Second World War approached. Throughout the war years, worship groups were held in the area around the University for mutual support and with volunteers participating in the nutrition and starvation experiments conducted there as Civilian Public Service projects. Some participants in these groups had opportunities to know some members of the well-established

Minneapolis Friends Meeting (affiliated with Iowa Yearly Meeting FUM), sharing common concerns for advancing peace, offering spiritual, and material help to men in Civilian Public Service or prison, and working together to improve the racial climate in the larger community.

These concerns were shared by seekers in Madison, Milwaukee, and the Twin Cities. All related to the American Friends Service Committee, the Fellowship of Reconciliation, and Friends Committee on National Legislation and were visited by outstanding Quaker leaders such as Kenneth Boulding, Elise Boulding, Joseph Havens, Douglas Steere, Teresina Rowell (Havens), and E. Raymond Wilson. Participation and support existed within each of these local meetings for many of the wartime undertakings of the national peace groups. (1)

1947–1960:
Northern Half-yearly Meeting is Established

Greater mobility following World War II set the stage for the establishment of Northern Half-yearly Meeting. In 1947, the worship group meeting at the University of Minnesota began meeting formally as the University Friends Meeting, changing its name to Church Street Meeting about 1952. (The name was changed again to Twin Cities Friends Meeting about 1962.) A preparative meeting relationship had existed with Minneapolis Friends Meeting from 1954–1955. The young meeting did not, however, feel in harmony with Iowa Yearly Meeting (Friends United Meeting) with which Minneapolis was then affiliated and chose to apply to Illinois Yearly Meeting (Friends General Conference) for membership and recognition as a monthly meeting. Illinois Yearly Meeting accepted this application in 1956 and Church Street Monthly Meeting took its place within Fox Valley Quarter, then including Chicago Fifty-Seventh Street, Downers Grove and Rock Valley, in Illinois, as well as Madison and Milwaukee in Wisconsin. (2)

The Early History of Northern Yearly Meeting

In July of 1960, the Fox Valley Quarter proposed to Illinois Yearly Meeting a change which would bring the growing Chicago area Friends into a newly formed Metropolitan Chicago General Meeting. This change would establish Northern Half-yearly Meeting for the Wisconsin and Minnesota meetings that were in development. Illinois Yearly Meeting accepted this proposal in August 1960. As new small meetings were formed, Friends in Northern Half-yearly Meeting felt empowered to take more confident steps in the nurture of one another. Most people looked forward to the "halfly" sessions as a time of spiritual renewal for all ages, sharing God's love deeply. For many Friends the "halfly" helped compensate for the isolation which they felt from the values of mainstream society. A Friend stated:

> *We didn't get together and "found" Quaker churches as missions. We found each other in our needs and concerns for peace, race relations and other social issues [as well as] our need to share parenting that emphasized these Quaker values.* (3)

1965–1975:
The Halfly Expands; Northern Yearly Meeting Established

From 1960 to 1965, following the pattern established in the Fox Valley Quarterly Meeting, responsibility for the spring and fall all-day Saturday meeting rotated among the three larger host cities. The average attendance was from 40–60 persons. Visitors stayed in the homes of Friends sharing hospitality and broadening their experience of Friends. Groups in Eau Claire, North Central Wisconsin (Wausau area), and Duluth-Superior formed and participated with the longer established meetings. (4)

Some far-sighted Friends took a major step forward when they initiated the first weekend camp format in the fall of 1965 at Camp

Waukaunda near Madison. The growth of Northern Half-yearly Meeting accelerated, as the needs of families for greater fellowship, worship, and education in Quakerism could be better met in a group residential setting. More than 140 persons attended! This fostered the establishment and nurturance of additional Friends groups in Beloit, Appleton/Green Bay/Fox Valley, and Stevens Point in Wisconsin and Northfield, Mankato, and Rochester in Minnesota. Members of Minneapolis Meeting also began attending informally at this time. A fair number of isolated Friends came to share in the Halfly as well.

Friends from Eau Claire, Milwaukee, Madison, and Oshkosh attended Illinois Yearly Meeting sessions each August, but unfortunately, distance prevented many Halfly Friends from attending. Gradually, the Halfly began filling a place in the lives of many of the meetings as if it were a yearly meeting. (5).

Between 1969 and 1971, informal discussions and several written proposals surfaced suggesting that the time was right to work toward becoming an independent association or yearly meeting. This movement gained some strength with the decision by Twin Cities Meeting in 1971 to resign its membership in Illinois Yearly Meeting. During these years, new meetings and attenders came to the Halfly from Ft. Atkinson, Wisconsin, and Decorah and Dubuque, Iowa.

In February 1974 Madison Meeting approved and circulated a minute suggesting: "...we should seek the assistance of Illinois Yearly Meeting...to explore the possibility of the establishment of a Northern Yearly Meeting..."(6)

Following careful deliberations during Halfly 1974 spring and fall sessions, a Structure Committee was appointed to develop such a proposal and to circulate it for discussion among the constituent meetings. (7)

Their report was presented to the Halfly Meeting for Business on September 13, 1975. On September 14, the Proposed Minute

The Early History of Northern Yearly Meeting

Establishing Northern Yearly Meeting was approved. (8) The change from the old to the new status felt like an evolutionary process. Illinois Yearly Meeting released the new Yearly Meeting as it celebrated its own centennial.

1975–1999:
Northern Yearly Meeting: The First 25 Years

The first 25 years witnessed vigorous growth in the size of the Northern Yearly Meeting gatherings. This growth was manifested by increases in attendance (325 in 1996), the establishment of new meetings and regional gatherings, and the expansion of the budget and extension of age diversity, as many of the early participants became "senior Friends." The increased growth brought increased responsibilities and increased complexity of organization. New committees developed to plan youth and adult programs, advancement and outreach, and to develop a newsletter. Responsibilities of both Executive Committee (now Interim Session) and Budget (now Finance) Committee have evolved greatly.

Many new meetings and worship groups have emerged: Bismarck, ND, Red River Valley ND/MN, Brainerd, Cannon Valley, Grand Rapids, Northern Lights (Bemidji), Prospect Hill, St. Cloud, St. Croix Valley, and Winona in Minnesota; Lake Superior (Marquette) and Keweenaw (Houghton), MI; Dodgeville, Kickapoo Valley, La Crosse, Interlake (Manitowoc), Sand Ridge, and Viroqua, in Wisconsin. New worship groups continued to arise, with many new seekers, along with Friends who relocated to the area. (9) Regional gatherings developed to meet needs for decentralized groupings for spiritual nurture, intergenerational, or youth nurture and fellowship.

A significant aspect of the early years of Northern Yearly Meeting was the development of some special connections for nurture, including Nightingales, Friendly Folk Dancers, the Friends for Lesbian and Gay Concerns, the Friends in Unity With Nature, and the Spiritual Nurture Program. The earliest of these, the Nightingales, began quite informally during the Halfly gatherings with a group of mothers who discovered they loved to sing together. They would meet to sing after the little ones were tucked in for the night. Others heard them, joined in, and made connections. The Nightingales became a vital part of the Halflys, and then the yearly meeting, and then were added to program plans, open to any who were willing to stay up late and sing along. Soon, three Nightingale weekends were added at rural locations accessible to the Twin Cities, Madison, and Milwaukee. Besides the pleasure provided by singing with other Friends, the Nightingales have contributed to deepening the lives of Friends of all ages, brought people together from small and large meetings, built a shared knowledge of hymns and songs which contribute to sung ministry in worship, and fostered the joy of singing and sharing the work of being together for the weekend.

Northern Yearly Meeting was only eleven years old when it came together to do the work to host a full Friends General Conference Gathering at Carlton College in Northfield, Minnesota. Including 2016, it has hosted four more Gatherings within our region, as well as a Caregivers Consultation one autumn. (10)

The Friendly Folk Dancers are an international Quaker ministry sprung from seeds sown and nurtured by the distinctive culture of Northern Yearly Meeting. Created in 1986, the group toured the east coast inviting Friends to the first Friends General Conference gathering hosted by NYM. The mission and message of the folk dancers has matured and solidified since that initial tour. They have carried their message across oceans, to several countries, more than 30 yearly meetings representing all major branches of Friends and an annual Section of Americas meeting of the FWCC. The Friendly Folk Dancers have carried a message of joy, peace, and international connection through dances of the world for all ages and abilities. Just as Friends seek to "'let their lives speak," the Friendly Folk Dancers seek to witness to the possibility of world concord with their physical prayer for peace. Fueled by the energy and creative spirit so characterized by Northern Yearly Meeting, the members of the Friendly Folk Dancers carry these characteristics cheerfully, dancing with that of God in all.

Development and maturation of NYM were given another boost when an adult spiritual nurture program was offered at a time separate from the annual yearly meeting sessions. The first weekend spiritual nurture retreat occurred in 1994 at St. Bedes Retreat Center near Eau Claire, Wisconsin. The retreat included guest leaders and established small core clusters of people who continued to connect after the retreat. Individuals in these groups developed various spiritual practices or disciplines such as prayer, journaling, worship-sharing together regularly, and spiritual friendships. The Spiritual Nurture Program had high expectations of time commitments, so it may appear that the overall number of people who participated was not great. One clear result has been deeper worship when the yearly meeting comes together; another positive result has been the spiritual development of more people who may be ready to carry leadership, ministry, and service forward within the yearly meeting.

Northern Welcomes Minneapolis Meeting

From 1937, and continuing through 1990, all meetings in NYM had been "new meetings." The character of these meetings was shaped by the sense of empowerment, which comes with the experience of discovering the Spirit alive within our worshiping communities and ourselves. Most individual members were convinced Friends, many quite new to the Society.

In 1986 Minneapolis Friends Meeting sent a letter asking for help in affiliating with a wider body of Friends. This prospective meeting brought a long history with Quakers, a large meeting community, a wide range of theological views, and a mix of birthright and convinced members. Some of the individual connections with Friends went back many years, some even generationally. Minneapolis had affiliated with Iowa Yearly Meeting in 1863 and was part of the 1877 separation in Iowa, which led to a pastoral form of organization in 1886. Iowa Yearly had begun participating in the Five Years Meeting (later Friends United Meeting) in 1902.

After considering various options, Minneapolis Monthly Meeting formally joined Northern Yearly Meeting in 1991.

One Annual Session

Northern Yearly Meeting had continued the two sessions per year format of the Halflys for the full meetings, as that had been so nurturing to the many new meetings. In 1991 that traditional two sessions format was changed to a single yearly session, an acknowledgment of supporting the fuller program responsibilities Northern was developing. In order to be more available to the larger constituency, NYM maintained the practice of alternating between the eastern and the western sides of the geographical region. The yearly meeting outgrew many camps and began to meet one year on a college campus and the next at a large camp. The Yearly Meeting was incorporated in Wisconsin in 1995. According to a statistical survey in 1986, there were about 475 active members and attenders within local meetings. A survey, completed in 2000, showed growth to 1200 members and attenders.

A Developing Relationship with El Salvador Yearly Meeting

The Friends World Committee for Consultation (FWCC) historically encouraged connections between yearly meetings, particularly in the north-south direction. The early roots of Northern Yearly Meeting's relationship with El Salvador Yearly Meeting (ESYM) began in the late 1970s when a Twin Cities Friend who had been born in El Salvador began to visit Friends there after connecting at an FWCC conference. Additional relationships were built over the years, involving Minneapolis and Cannon Valley Friends who shared public health concerns with Salvadoran Friends. Physicians in Minneapolis Meeting who were representatives to FWCC learned of the shortage of medical supplies in El Salvador, and began donating supplies and funds to meet that need, encouraging others to do likewise.

In 1998 FWCC moved to lay down the International Quaker Aid program, which was supporting the ESYM clinic and primary schools. The Twin Cities Friends Social Action Committee suggested a sister yearly meeting relationship with ESYM and support of the clinic and schools. After the yearly meeting clerks exchanged correspondence, an agreement was reached in 2000 to form an alliance for mutual benefit. The first official exchange of representatives at annual sessions occurred the following year.

After the 2001 earthquake, Salvadoran Friends provided homes and an education through Friends Schools for a number of orphans. Northern Yearly Meeting Friends committed some financial resources to relief efforts and continued further intervisitation and collaboration.

Salvadoran Friends have offered a variety of interest groups, discussions, and cultural activities, and led worship on several occasions during regular annual session visits.

Many close, personal ties have been forged as a result, and many NYM Friends appreciate the spiritual depth of worship with Salvadoran Friends. However, Salvadorans' difficulty in obtaining visas, particularly young Salvadorans, has limited their number at NYM annual sessions.

In 2004 the first of several NYM youth groups went to El Salvador where they experienced spiritual, social and touristic activities hosted by Salvadoran Friends. Several pairs of NYM volunteers have taught English for a month in the ESYM Friends schools Soyapango and San Ignacio. Many NYM Friends have donated scholarship funds to the schools.

Through continuing visits and increased communication at the leadership level the yearly meetings have strengthened bonds of love and fellowship across cultural and religious differences. The relationship has provided both opportunities for reflection and growth, and opportunities to serve. The Good News of Jesus shared by Salvadoran Friends, and the abiding spiritual hospitality they have offered has deepened and enriched the spiritual lives of NYM Friends.

Nurturing our Youth

One major factor in holding attendance of NYM sessions steady has been the continuing development of the Children and Youth program. As our twice a year sessions moved from camp to campus, people looked for ways and space to provide activities that would support family attendance. Teen programs were the first to be offered, separate from the general childcare spaces. As attendance numbers increased, our larger sites also provided spaces for a variety of children and youth activities to be offered. Program planners found families were eager for children to have activities that reflected the theme of the session for all. The yearly meeting was growing in size overall; many of the local meetings, however, were quite small, with only a few children, or sometimes none. Parents were looking for resources, help to name and live our Quaker values, and a place for families to simply have fun together.

The Children and Youth Committee came to clearness that spiritual nurture via weekend events was needed for our youth, and that a steady organizer was needed to provide a more year-round program. In 2007 NYM took the big step of approving the hiring of our first paid youth organizer. The details were in place to hire a teen coordinator in 2009.

The Early History of Northern Yearly Meeting

Northern Yearly Meeting has provided rich opportunities for worship, business, education, and fellowship for participants from youngest to oldest. We continue listening to the voice of the Inner Guide. A vital, creative energy has been characteristic of the experience of Northern Yearly Meeting during the last 40 years. We pray that we will continue to be led on this corporate spiritual journey into the future.

References:

1. Sources for this section:
    Madison Meeting: Francis Hole, *A Preliminary Historical Record of the Madison Monthly Meeting of the Religious Society of Friends,* unpublished manuscript, 1960, pp. 6–9 and 14–27.

    Milwaukee Meeting: Bill Brown, *A Brief History of Milwaukee Friends Meeting: Fifty Years of Quaker Presence in Milwaukee,* 1991.

    Minneapolis Meeting: Gordon Coffin, written, undated reminiscences (probably transcribed during the 1970s).

    Thomas E. Drake, "Quakers in Minnesota," *Minnesota History* (September 1937).

    Alexina Gray, *Memories of Early Days in Minneapolis,* 1963, unpublished ms.

    Edith H. Jones, *History of Minneapolis Friends Meeting, 1863–1963,* Unpublished manuscript.

    John Parker, *Minneapolis Friends: A Brief History,* 1981, unpublished manuscript.

    Twin Cities Friends Meeting: Raquel Wood, telephone interviews with John and Mary Phillips, Alex Stach and Beverly White, 1996. Taped interviews with Howard Lutz, 1976. Informal discussions with others over the years.

2. As there is a great deal of variation in the status of meetings when they came into the community of Northern Yearly Meeting in its various stages, Appendix D has been developed. It lists the years and means by which the meetings formally became "Monthly Meetings" and joined Northern Yearly Meeting.
3. Barbara Greenler to Raquel K. Wood, personal correspondence, March 1996.
4. Raquel K. Wood, *Northern Yearly Meeting: A Tenth Anniversary Commemoration*, 1985.
5. At various times among some of the constituent meetings, and sometimes spilling over into the Halfly, Friends have felt it appropriate to act "as if" there were in fact a monthly meeting because of great distances or because there was sufficient experience within the meeting or because Friends felt they were a monthly meeting in all respects already. It is a confidence built on having to take responsibility when there seems to be no readily established way of accomplishing the goal.
6. The complete text of the minute reads:

It is the sense of this (Ministry & Counsel) Committee that we should seek the assistance of Illinois Yearly Meeting and of its constituent Monthly Meetings in Wisconsin to explore the possibility over the next two or three years of the establishment of a Northern Yearly Meeting: and that, to that end, the Northern Half-yearly Meeting be considered as a "preparative meeting" through which the response of local Meetings to such a development could be weighed.

We express the hope that Illinois Yearly Meeting might regard this development as an appropriate outgrowth of its first century, and respond in the conviction that the formation of a Northern Yearly Meeting is fully consis-

tent with the celebration of the centennial observance planned in the year ahead.
—Madison Monthly Meeting, February 1974, Wood.

7. Members of the Structure Committee were: Lila and Elliot Cornell, clerks, Paul Bartoo, Phyllis Berentsen, Betty Boardman, Nancy Breitsprecher, Jeff Haines, Ron Mattson, Rosalie Wahl, and Stan White.
8. The Structure and Function chapter of this Faith and Practice contains the complete text of the Establishing Minute.
9. Appendix D lists all the meetings and dates of their affiliation through 2000, which we take to be the conclusion of our early history.
10. Elaine Carte, *Our Meeting and Affiliation: A Short History*, ca 1987. Elaine Carte, *Minneapolis Meeting: A Quick Tour of the Past*, 1996 (full text in Appendix F).

See Appendices

Appendix D: Monthly Meetings of NYM, Chronological Order of Joining Through 2000
Appendix E: Clerks of Northern Halfly and Yearly, 1960-2000
Appendix F: Full text of *Minneapolis Meeting: A Quick Tour of the Past*, included because the history of Minneapolis Meeting is unique within Northern Yearly Meeting.

Approved 2005, updated 2016

Faith and Practice

RESOURCES

Quaker Quotes

The Faith and Practice Committee received many more submissions and quotes than we could include in our chapters. We wanted and wrote a chapter on *Friends and Money* but it never was sent to constituent meetings for input and never submitted for approval. The committee wanted to include something about Quaker humor. After some discernment we decided to add a chapter with some of the material sent to us but not used and include some comments on *Friends and Money* and humor. What follows is but a fraction of the material received.

> *How healing [it is] to come into the Religious Society of Friends, whose founder saw clearly that the Light of God is not limited to the male half of the human race. Membership and participation have helped me grow toward wholeness.*
> —Elizabeth Watson, 1975, in *Faith and Practice*, North Pacific Yearly Meeting, 1986. p. 34.
>
> *It is easy for Friends to believe in nonviolence, [Dunbar] explained, because in their own homes and meetings and schools they are protected from the rough life most poor people know. Friends in fact do live nonviolently among*

themselves....but they do not always develop enough concern about the ugly world outside.
—Barrington Dunbar, *A Quaker Speaks from the Black Experience: the Life and Selected Writings of Barrington Dunbar*, ed. James Fletcher and Carleton Mabee, New York Yearly Meeting, 1979, p. 18.

Preaching nonviolence to those victimized by violent situations is a palliative that will not heal hate, fear and distrust. It is only as we are able to help people to live nonviolently by bringing them into nonviolent relationships that healing and transformation will take place.
—Barrington Dunbar, p. 57.

The Quaker Testimony is that Christ is in each one of us, his spirit is in each one of us. What I have been trying to show—especially since I met Dorothy Day—is that Christ is with us as a living force. Grasping the fact that this is in each of us would prohibit killing, prohibit war and destruction. It would establish the sacredness, the sanctity of human life.
—Philip Harnden, *Letting That Go, Keeping This: The Spiritual Pilgrimage of Fritz Eichenberg* (Pendle Hill Pamphlet #353, 2001), p. 28.

I have never been without my criticisms of Quakerism. I find Quakers in general too polite, too genteel! I think they would rather have the American Friends Service Committee respond to crisis than respond themselves.
—Philip Harnden, p. 24.

Still, the Peace Testimony calls me always to look first to love: to open to others with a spirit of understanding, forgiveness and reconciliation. I cannot do this by myself. Living the Peace Testimony requires that I live from

Quaker Quotes

its Source: that I stand in the Light, see the truth of what I am and yield to the Divine Presence. Only then may I hope to "live in the virtue of that life and power that takes away the occasion of all wars."
—Steve Smith, *Living In Virtue, Declaring Against War* (Pendle Hill Pamphlet, #378, 2005), p.34,

True simplicity should connote not poverty but, rather, a richness of spirit, a joy in living, the nurturing of creativity, sensitivity to the natural world, and love for all creatures. As an expression of this love, this true simplicity, we must then, too, commit ourselves to building a more equitable world—a world in which this simplicity may thrive and be enjoyed by everyone...
—Ann Kriebel, "What is Simplicity?" *Friends Journal* (December 13, 1984).

We [Quakers] are called as watercolors are called across a page: not a simple, straight line nor one shape, but many colors with different densities of light and overlapping pigment, rarely tidy.
—John Calvi, "A Call to Spiritual Discipline," *Friends Journal* (May 2007), p. 16.

Prayer for Simplicity

That we may learn to live on less, take
no more from Gaia than she can safely spare,
leave for other creatures everywhere
and for the future what they'll need to make
their lives complete—this is now our prayer,
dear Christ. Nor can we safely wait to learn
this hard lesson, for every daily turn
of Gaia finds her needing to repair
more wounds our wasteful ways inflict. We mourn

those wounds, dear Christ, and humbly pray that you help simplify our wantings and undo our folly. So may the world be reborn a new Jerusalem where everyone delights to share all blessings under the sun.
—David Langworthy, *Among Friends: Poems,* privately published and copyrighted by David Langworthy, 2003, p. 139.

This is my commandment, that you love one another as I have loved you. No one has greater love than this, to lay down one's life for one's friends. You are my friends if you do what I command you. I do not call you servants any longer...but I have called you friends...You did not choose me but I chose you. And I appointed you to go and bear fruit...I am giving you these commands so that you may love one another.
—John 15:12–17 (NRSV)

We do not ever get to see all the flowers in the world; only a few. We do not get to see all the treasures in people's hearts, even though every person has a treasure. It is as if the Presence said, "I do not let you see more than a few treasures. But from the sample that you do see, you know that what I give you is a fine treasure. That is what I am like." Yes, it is good. (#45)
—Francis D. Hole and Ellie Shacter, *A Little Journal of Devotions out of Quaker Worship: An experiment with 104 entries across two thousand miles* (Philadelphia: Quaker Press, 2001. Madison WI: The Friends Press, 1995).

Live in love, awe and gratitude. Love neighbor, self, plant, animal, rock, moon, stars, sun equally. Do not be troubled. Release attachments. Notice your capacity to

Quaker Quotes

be happy and to laugh with the Divine Being, in whom
you swim and breath. (#88)
—Francis D. Hole and Ellie Shacter

The earth beneath the feet of all runners and walkers
Declare the glory of God, our Cherisher!
The roots of trees and grasses, the mole
And all organisms in the rich realm of darkness...
These are God's handiwork.
Our life in the realm of sunlight
Is upheld by the vital earth. God made it so.
All creatures that live on the land depend on the soil,
Which is like a strong parent,
Providing for all peoples and
All creatures that live above the waters.
Praise be to the holy ground that is softly under our feet!
Praise be to God who has blessed the living carpet
That He has spread for our walking,
In the days of our living in the flesh,
And unto which our rich residues will return.
—An original Psalm by Francis Hole, inspired by Psalm
19, From *Soil Survey Horizons* (Spring 1988).

"How is it to be so old?" [Emilia (then in her 90s) was asked by a young student after a talk she'd given.] "Well, I'll tell you. I've gone to many kinds of schools, but of all the courses in the university of life, the course in old age is the hardest, the one with the most lessons to learn. Your own generation is gone. You can no longer count on your intellect or your memory. Your hearing lets you down. You can't keep track of things and you're constantly misplacing them. But you learn so much. You learn to accept help and to remember with your heart. To live always with the generations that went before, with those alive

now, and with the generations to come – all that we must surely learn. In one way life is like a mountain climb, and we keep going steadily upward toward our death. And when we meet it, when Brother Death comes and gives us permission to go on across the frontier, then we must meet him with thankfulness, only thankfulness."
—Emilia Fogelklou, *Reality and Radiance: Selected Autobiographical Works of Emilia Fogelklou,* translated by Howard Lutz (Friends United Press, 1986), p.63.

Let us review the lessons I have learned from those various people:
1. *Rather than run from those in conflict, let us visit them.*
2. *Do not let danger deter us.*
3. *Let us confront the violence in the United States so that we lessen the wars, conflicts, and economic exploitation that the United States brings to other parts of the world.*
4. *Let love replace hatred. Let us restore that of God in those who have done bad things.*
5. *Let us address the roots of violence in order to reduce societal and domestic violence.*
6. *Let us bring enemies together to "look each other in the eye."*
7. *Let us stop judging people as "good" or "bad" but answer to that of God in absolutely everyone.*
8. *And the unifying lesson:*
9. *Let us dwell deep that we may feel and understand the spirits of people.*
—David Zarembka of the Friends Peace Teams and African Great Lakes Initiative, 59th annual John Woolman Memorial Lecture at Mount Holly NJ in October 2006, Conclusion. Healing from Slavery, War, and Genocide:

Quaker Quotes

Lessons from John Woolman and Friends in Rwanda and Burundi. Entire article: http://www.aglifpt.org

Have salt in yourselves. Let your words be few and seasoned that they may be savory. Watch over one another in love, walk in wisdom and sobriety, gravity, sincerity, purity, and cleanness. And the Lord keep you all in his fear and in his obedience now and evermore.
—George Fox, Epistle 22, 1652, as published in "The Power of the Lord is Over All," *The Pastoral Letters of George Fox*, Introduced and edited by T. Canby Jones (Friends United Press, Richmond, Indiana, 1989), p. 16.

Worship, which is as necessary for full and complete life, as breathing...It cannot be delegated. It is both individual and corporate...Each one...helps to produce an atmosphere and spirit in which all the others who compose the waiting group are strengthened and assisted...
—Rufus Jones, *The Quaker's Faith*, FGC pamphlet, 1972.

Friends and Money

For where your treasure is, there your heart will be also.
—Matthew 6:21 (NRSV)

People have a surprising amount of energy for what happens to dollars and cents, even small amounts of them.
—John Kraft, Northern Yearly Meeting, 2005.

Northern Yearly Meeting follows a specific budgeting process and keeps fiscal accounts in order to help NYM to:
• *Carry out God's work in the world, as we have collectively discerned it;*
• *Nurture and deepen our faithfulness to the Spirit, among both adults and children;*

- *Nurture and support our constituent meetings and worship groups;*
- *Gather together each year in work and fellowship, and nurture relationships among Friends.*

—Budget Committee report to NYM, 2001.

Wealth desired for its own sake obstructs the increase of virtue...
—John Woolman, "A Plea for the Poor" in *The Journal and Major Essays of John Woolman*, Ed. Phillips P. Moulton, Friends United Press, Richmond, Indiana, 1971. p. 238.

Here we have a prospect of one common interest from which our own is inseparable—that to turn all we possess into the channel of universal love becomes the business of our lives.
—Woolman, p.241.

It is not enough to be generous, and give alms. The enlarged soul, the true philanthropist, is compelled by Christian principle to look...to the duty of considering the causes and sources of poverty. We must consider how much we have done toward causing it.
—Lucretia Mott, *Lucretia Mott Speaking*, 1860, compiled by Margaret Hope Bacon (Pendle Hill Pamphlet #234, 1980), p. 18.

A Little Quaker Humor

Stephen Cary tells the following story of his years at Haverford College in the mid 1930s:

Even the college's "Fifth day Meeting" which all students were required to attend, was not exempt from un-Quakerly behavior. Its pillar was philosopher Rufus Jones,

Quaker Quotes

who sat on the facing benches and was so regularly called by the Lord to preach that we heathen organized a weekly pool: maximum number of participants, 15; entry fee, 25 cents. Each entrant recorded a time, at 30-second intervals when he predicted the great man would rise to preach. An official timekeeper was named, whose ruling was final in a winner-take-all contest. Rufus never knew how much rode on when the Lord called him.
—Stephen G. Cary, *The Intrepid Quaker: One Man's Quest for Peace*, edited by Alison Anderson and Jack Coleman (Pendle Hill Publications), p.11–12

At the same Haverford College, some years later the students began chafing against the required attendance at the Thursday morning Meeting for Worship. The students showed their displeasure by reading, sometimes making rude noises, being restless and looking bored. William Bacon Evans was frequently seen on campus. Bacon Evans wore plain dress and used the plain speech (thee and thou) of early Friends. Bacon Evans attending one of these worships finally rose and spoke: "Two skeletons were hanging in a closet. One skeleton said to the other: 'If we had any guts we would get out of here.'"
—Anna Cox Brinton, *The Wit and Wisdom of William Bacon Evans* (Pendle Hill Pamphlet #146, 1966), p. 39.

Rufus Jones startled Haverford Meeting once when he rose to speak: "This morning my daughter Mary Hoxie said to me, 'Father, I could be more sure you were inspired if you weren't inspired so regularly.'"
—Eric W. Johnson, *Quaker Meeting: A Risky Business* (Pittsburg, PA: Dorrance Publishing Co., 1991), p 53.

Raquel Wood tells the story that when Northern Yearly Meet-

ing was still a half-yearly, we met in 1964 at the Historical Society of Wausau, Wisconsin. The hosts had a pet mynah bird who would screech "Historical Society!" whenever the telephone rang. Friends discovered the bird had a larger vocabulary. A Friend rose during Meeting for Worship and began to speak only to have the bird call out "Aw Shut Up."
 —Northern Yearly Meeting 1985, Tenth Anniversary Commemorative, Raquel Wood, p. 2; permission of the author.

When Northern Yearly Meeting started a spiritual nurture program, the program involved weekend retreats. Rich Van Dellen recalls at one of those retreats we were warmly greeted on entering the main building of the retreat center with the sign "WELCOME QUACKERS."

Tom Mullen, a popular professor at Earlham School of Religion, was to give a plenary address at one of the annual Friends General Conference Gatherings. He was from a Quaker pastoral tradition but decided since he was to address unprogrammed Friends he would let the Spirit guide what he was to say. As he waited on stage to be introduced nothing was coming to him. He started to sweat not knowing what he was to say. Then he got a nudge and thought the Spirit was finally speaking to him as to what to say. The message he got: "Tom Mullen, thee is unprepared."

The oft-repeated saying that Quakers do not sing well because they are always looking ahead to see if they agree with the words was certainly not true at NYM. Long before we became a Yearly Meeting, a group would sing long into the night after the evening program. They became known as The Nightingales. Barbara Greenler, Rosalie Wahl, and other founding women, affectionately called collectively the Celestial Mamas! exhorted singers to memorize the songs—get your nose out of the hymnbook and look at each other. They even gathered together some of their favorite songs and printed them in a pamphlet. The word was that you had to stay and sing until after midnight to be a true Nightingale. One man, quite tired before the midnight hour, quoted from a Whittier hymn, "Let sense be dumb, let flesh retire." He retired. It remains unclear whether he was granted honorary Nightingale status anyway.

—Recollections of Rich Van Dellen from several people, with the Whittier Hymn Quote from Chuck Fager, *Quakers Are Hilarious!* (Kimo Press, 2013), p 12

Seen on a T-shirt: "For God so Loved The World, That She Did NOT Send A Committee." Jane 3:16

—Chuck Fager, *Quakers Are Hilarious!* (Kimo Press 2013), p 13.

Quaker Resources

Blogs

Craig Bennett, British, transitionquaker.blogspot.co.uk.

John Calvi, healer, www.johncalvi.com.

Exploring Quaker Spirituality, Faith & Practice, throughtheflamingsword.wordpress.com.

Marcelle Martin, Quaker spirituality, a wholeheart.com.

Liz Oppenheimer, Quaker thinker & activist, thegoodraisedup. blogspot.com.

A list of Quaker blogs is available at http://Quaker.zebby.org/.

Books
Introductions/Overviews

Britain Yearly Meeting. *Quaker Faith & Practice.* Five editions. London: Quaker Books, 2005. Also on line at qfp. quaker.org.uk.

Fager, Chuck. *Without Apology: The Heroes, The Heritage and the Hope of Liberal Quakerism.* Bellefonte, PA: Kimo Press, 1996.

Gorman, George H. *The Amazing Fact of Quaker Worship*. London: Quaker Home Service, 1979.

Gulley, Phillip. *Living the Quaker Way: Timeless Wisdom for a Better Life Today*. New York: Random House, 2013.

Gywn, Douglas. *A Sustainable Life: Quaker Faith and Practice in the Renewal of Creation*. Philadelphia: Quaker Press of FGC (Friends General Conference), 2014.

Navias, Mathilda. *Quaker Process: For Friends on the Benches*. Philadelphia: Friends Publishing, Inc., 2012.

Spears, Joanne & Larry. *Friendly Faith and Practice Study Guide*. Philadelphia: Quaker Books, 1997.

West, Jessamyn. *The Quaker Reader*. Wallingford, PA: Pendle Hill Publications, 1992. A collection of Quaker authors over the years, selected and introduced by the author.

History

Bacon, Margaret Hope. *Mothers of Feminism: The Story of Quaker Women in America*. San Francisco: Harper and Row, 1986.

Barbour, Hugh and J. William Frost. *The Quakers*. Denominations in America Series. Westport, CT: Greenwood Press, 1988.

Kunze, Bonnelyn Young. *Margaret Fell and the Rise of Quakerism*. Stanford, CA: Stanford University Press, 1994

Newman, Daisy. *A Procession of Friends: Quakers in America*. Richmond, IN: Friends United Press, 1972.

Punshon, John. *Portrait in Grey: A Short History of the Quakers*. London : Quaker Books, 1984.

Classics

Fox, George. *Truth of the Heart: An Anthology of George Fox 1624–1691*. Edited by Rex Ambler. Quaker Books, 2001.

Boulding, Kenneth. *The Naylor Sonnets*. Quaker Books and Friends United Press, 2007.

Brinton, Howard H. *Friends for 350 Years: The History and Beliefs of the Society of Friends*. Wallingford, PA. Pendle Hill Publications, 2002.

Penn, William. *Twenty-First Century Penn*. Edited by Paul Buckley. Richmond, IN: ESR, 2003.

Peterson, Eugene H. *The Message: The Bible in Contemporary Language*. Colorado Springs, CO: NavPress Publishing Group, 2002.

Woolman, John. *The Journal and Major Essays of John Woolman*. Edited by Phillips P. Moulton. New York: Oxford University Press, 1971.

Spiritual Journeys

Boulding, Elise. *Born Remembering*. Pendle Hill Pamphlet #200. Wallingford, PA: Pendle Hill, 1975.

Buckley, Paul & Angell, Stephen W., eds. *The Quaker Bible Reader*. Richmond, IN: Earlham School of Religion, 2006.

Fogelklou, Emilia. *Reality and Radiance: Selected Autobiographical Works of Emilia Fogelklou*. Introduction and translation by Howard Lutz. Forward by Douglas Steere. Richmond, IN: Friends United Press, 1986.

Kerman, Cynthia Earl. *Creative Tension: The Life and Thought of Kenneth Boulding.* Ann Arbor, MI: University of Michigan Press, 1974.

Loring, Patricia. *Listening Spirituality: Vol 1 – Personal Spiritual Practices Among Friends.* Washington, DC: Openings Press, 1997.

Kelly, Thomas R. *A Testament of Devotion.* New York: Harper & Row, 1941. This edition also includes a biographical memoir of Thomas Kelly by Douglas V. Steere.

Steere, Douglas, ed. *Quaker Spirituality.* New York: Paulist Press, 1983.

Watson, Elizabeth. *Guests of My Life.* Burnsville, NC: Celo Press, 1979. Details her personal growth through Emily Dickinson, Rainer Maria Rilke, Katherine Mansfield, Rabindranath Tagore, Alan Paton, and Walt Whitman.

Novels

Allen, Irene. *Quaker Testimony. Quaker Witness. Quaker Silence. Quaker Indictment.* New York: St. Martin's Press, various dates.

de Hartog, Jan. *The Peaceable Kingdom.* New York: Harper & Row, 1975. The first of a trilogy.

West, Jessamyn. *Except for Me and Thee.* 1 of 3. New York: Avon, 1969.

Quaker Action

American Friends Service Committee. *SPEAK TRUTH TO POWER: A Quaker Search for an Alternative to Violence.* Philadelphia: American Friends Service Committee, 1955. A Study of International Conflict.

Quaker Resources

(Bayard Rustin was the main author, writing for a committee.)

Boardman, Elizabeth Jelinek. *The Phoenix Trip: Notes on a Quaker Mission to Haiphong*. Burnsville, NC: Celo Press, 1985.

Brinton, Howard H. *Guide to Quaker Practice*. Pendle Hill Pamphlet #20. Wallingford, PA: Pendle Hill, 1955.

Fager, Chuck, ed. *Friends & the Vietnam War: Papers and Presentations from a Pendle Hill Conference*. Wallingford, PA: Pendle Hill Press, 1998.

Houtman, Jacqueline, Walter Naegle, and Michael G. Long. *Bayard Rustin: The Invisible Activist*. Philadelphia, PA: Quaker Press of FGC, 2014.

Irving, Nancy, Vicki Hain Poorman, and Margaret Fraser, eds. *Friends Peace Witness in a Time of Crisis*. Philadelphia: Friends World Committee for Consultation, 2005.

Jonas, Gerald. *On Doing Good: The Quaker Experiment*. New York: Charles Scribner's Sons, 1971.

Jones, Rufus M. *The Faith and Practice of the Quakers*. Richmond, IN: Friends United Press, 2007. (Originally published 1927.)

Sibley, Mulford Q., ed. *The Quiet Battle: Writings on the Theory and Practice of Non-Violent Resistance*. Boston: Beacon Press, 1963.

Simple Living Collective. *Taking Charge: Achieving Personal & Political Change Through Simple Living*. San Francisco: American Friends Service Committee, 1977.

Periodicals

Friends Journal – a monthly magazine of Quaker thought and life based in Philadelphia. It includes QuakerSpeak videos, article previews and a blog. See http://www.friendsjournal.org.

Pendle Hill Pamphlet series, Wallingford, Pennsylvania. For 80 years Pendle Hill has expanded understanding of Quaker life and witness through publications, particularly its pamphlet series. http://www.pendlehill.org.

What Canst Thou Say, A periodical about mystical experiences of Friends http://www.whatcanstthousay.org/subscribe/.

Websites

Northern Yearly Meeting – The regional body of Quaker Meetings affiliated with Friends General Conference, mostly in Minnesota and Wisconsin. See http://www.northernyearlymeeting.org.

Friends General Conference – The national organization of affiliated yearly meetings which offers services and resources to individuals, Quaker Meetings, & others. See http://www.fgcquaker.org.

American Friends Service Committee Quaker peace and justice organization based in Philadelphia which (with British Friends Service Committee) won Nobel Peace Prize in 1947. See afsc.org, or for local project, the Twin Cities Healing Justice Project, afsc.org/office/st-paul-minn.

Friends Committee on National Legislation (FCNL)– The lobbying arm of Quakers in the USA & grounded in pragmatic work with Congress. See fcnl.org.

Quaker Resources

Friends for Lesbian, Gay, Bisexual, Transgender and Queer Concerns – A North American Quaker faith community that affirms that of God in all people. See flgbtqc.org.

Friends World Committee for Consultation (FWCC) – The international collaboration of all Quaker yearly meetings from all varieties of Friends and some independent yearly meetings. It seeks to provide information about and promote connections between all Quakers. fwccworld.org.

Camp Woodbrooke – A Quaker-sponsored camp near Richland Center, Wisconsin that provides simple outdoor living in non-competitive, ecology-oriented camp offerings for families and youth 7 to 15. See http://www.campwoodbrooke.org.

Quaker Earthcare Witness – A network of spiritually centered North American Quakers who integrate environmental concerns with Friends testimonies. See quakerearthcare.org.

Alternatives to Violence Project – AVP is an international all-volunteer effort to help people learn alternatives to violence in their lives. Applications of pacifism. See avpusa.org. AVP operates under Friends for a Non-Violent World.

Friends for a Non-Violent World – Quaker-founded organization in St. Paul, Minnesota that demonstrates the power of transformation at personal, community and institutional level, particularly through the Minnesota Alternatives to Violence Project. See http://www.fnvw.org/.

Friends School of Minnesota – An independent K – 8 progressive school in St. Paul. See https://fsmn.org.

Northern Spirit Radio – Audio service that promotes world healing. See http://www.northernspiritradio.org.

NontheistFriends.org – presents the work of Friends (Quakers) who are more concerned with the natural than the supernatural, See nontheistfriends.org.

Quaker Universalist Fellowship – a Quaker network for exploring diverse spiritual paths, which includes Quaker Universalist Voice. See universalistfriends.org.

Voices of Friends is the website for the Wider Quaker Fellowship materials, made available by Friends World Committee on Consultation. See http://www.voicesoffriends.org/.

Appendices

Appendix A: Original Minute Establishing Northern Yearly Meeting

Recognizing the joy and celebration experienced each time we gather together for fellowship and as a worshipping community, individual Friends and Friends within several monthly meetings in the Wisconsin-Minnesota area announce the birth of a new entity within the Religious Society of Friends: NORTHERN YEARLY MEETING.

In drawing together, we subscribe to what earlier Friends wrote about the nature of a yearly meeting: it "shall be a free association of Monthly Meetings for mutual support and consultation and for furthering such concerns as its members have in common. Its relation to a Monthly Meeting is consultative and not authoritative."

With these understandings of ourselves and the nature of a yearly meeting, we therefore establish Northern Yearly Meeting of the Religious Society of Friends with the following structure:
Item I: Name.
The name of this body shall be Northern Yearly Meeting of the Religious Society of Friends.
Item II: Membership.
Membership in Northern Yearly Meeting shall be comprised of Monthly Meetings which choose to affiliate and are approved by

Meeting for Business. Member Monthly Meetings may also hold membership in another Yearly Meeting.

Item III: Participation.

All programs and events of Northern Yearly Meeting are open to any individual, worship group, or Monthly Meeting wishing to participate.

Item IV: Officers.

Officers for Northern Yearly Meeting shall be:

- **Clerk** – who shall preside over business sessions and shall prepare the business agenda.
- **Assistant Clerk** – who shall preside in the Clerk's absence.
- **Recording Clerk** – who shall keep accurate records and minutes as needed.
- **Treasurer** – who shall collect, record, and disperse all funds as directed by Meeting for Business.
- **Assistant Treasurer** – who shall operate under the direction of the Treasurer.

Officers and terms of office shall be determined by Meeting for Business.

Item V: Committees.

All committees shall be established by the Meeting for Business for not more than one year.

Item VI: Sessions.

Northern Yearly Meeting shall meet twice during each calendar year.

Item VII: Finances.

Meeting for Business shall determine financial needs, share these needs with individuals and Monthly Meetings, and hope for the best.

Item VIII : Affiliations.

Meeting for Business shall determine with which Friends organizations Northern Yearly Meeting shall affiliate.

Appendices

Item IX: Establishment of Monthly Meetings.

Application (s) for Monthly Meeting status shall be considered in Meeting for Business upon the recommendation of either a member Monthly Meeting or a committee appointed by Northern Yearly Meeting.

Item X: Method of Operation.

Northern Yearly Meeting shall conduct its Meeting for Business after the manner of Friends.

Appendix B: Why Develop a Faith and Practice

In 1994, after twenty years of discussing the proposal, Northern Yearly Meeting (NYM) appointed a standing committee to create a Faith and Practice. Those writing this purpose agreed to become the committee, on behalf of everyone in Northern Yearly Meeting.

We Believe That:

- Friends in Northern Yearly Meeting are a happy people who have a passion for each other and are ready to affirm the bond that exists between us;
- We are developing a statement of what we in NYM believe about our relation to God and how we can work together in love to do what God wants us to do;
- Developing a Faith and Practice statement, a rite of passage for any yearly meeting, will help NYM mature as an organization;
- A Faith and Practice is the "spine" of a yearly meeting that keeps it standing straight – it is the 'modus operandi' of our Quaker communal practice;
- The process of creating a Faith and Practice will help us grow together as we seek to know and document what we believe to be God's way for NYM;
- There is continuing revelation;
- Northern Yearly Meeting in its uniqueness has ideas to contribute to contemporary Quaker thought as we discover and articulate our uniqueness.

Therefore We Created a Process To:

- work out and state our ways of being and doing together;
- generative wide discussion within NYM as we struggle to articulate our uniquenesses, our beliefs and practices;

Appendices

- engage the whole of the Yearly Meeting in Spirit-led decision-making process about matters of deep spiritual importance;
- explore our differences so that we may learn to live together in love, in spite of those differences as we learn to resolve differences;
- provide opportunity for NYM to explore our faith and the way what we believe balances with what we do;
- practice listening fully to God speaking through each of us.

So That We Will Have a Book That Will:

- remind us of our own ways of being and acting together in NYM;
- be a teaching device for people who join with us to learn about what we believe and do to carry out God's ways in the Northern Plains;
- minimize misunderstandings and disagreements within the yearly meeting;
- help us to commit ourselves and be accountable to agreed upon standards;
- help us administer communal relations fairly and consistently in the way that is best for NYM;
- help us understand what we are doing and why we are doing it;
- explain to others how we work;
- help newcomers and children understand our religion – who we are, what we believe, what we do and why we do it;
- help us maintain the traditions of Friends in NYM;
- be a ready reference for individual Friends groups in the upper Midwest.

Purpose of a Faith and Practice for Northern Yearly Meeting:

The ultimate purpose is to have a book that defines the practic-

es (Faith and Practice) of the Religious Society of Friends as experienced and lived by Friends and monthly meetings and worship groups in Northern Yearly Meeting.
The book could be used as:

- devotional reading;
- a resource for NYM constituent groups on procedures, such as marriage, clearness committees, membership, etc.;
- a source of information for newcomers and seekers;
- gifts for new members, high school, and college graduates;
- a reference for Quaker beliefs and practices.

The process in developing this book will:

- involve the entire Yearly Meeting;
- be Spirit-led;
- enable NYM and its monthly meetings to define what practices and beliefs we have contributed or can contribute to the larger body of Quaker thought;
- ask members and attenders to examine their beliefs;
- allow differences among us to surface so they can be examined in the light of the Spirit, discussed, and struggled over; hoping with Divine assistance to reach a sense of the Meeting.

Appendix C: Marriage Certificates, Possible Wordings

Couples may review the wording with their arrangements committee. The wording of the vows is important to include, as the signatures are witnessing what has been said. Many current certificates do not include the names of the parents, or the county of residence.

These are the traditional words:

WHEREAS, (name_____), County of (name_____) and State of (name), son of (name_____) and (name_____), County of (name_____), State of (name)_____ and (name_____), daughter of (name_____) and (name_____), having made known their intentions of marriage with each other, in a Monthly Meeting of the Religious Society of Friends, held at (name_____), (name_____), and having consent of their parents, their proposals were allowed by this Meeting, These are to certify that for the full accomplishment of their intentions, this _____ day of _____, in the year of our Lord _____, they appeared in an appointed meeting of the Religious Society of Friends, held at (place_____), where they took each other by the hand and publicly declared that, in the presence of the Lord, they did promise, with Divine assistance, to be loving and faithful to one another as long as they both shall live.

As a further confirmation thereof, they did then and thereto sign their names:

_____ _____

And we, whose names are hereunto affixed, being present at this marriage, have as witnesses thereto subscribed our names.

Appendix D: Monthly Meetings of NYM, Chronological Order of Joining through 2000

Status indicates the year this group became a monthly meeting

Meeting	Began	Status	Description
Minneapolis (MN)	1852	1863	Member Iowa -FUM 1863–1982; NYM 1991
Madison (WI)	1934	1937	Joined Friends Fellowship Council, ILYM 1945; NYM #1
Milwaukee (WI)	1937	1950	Preparative under Evanston, NYM #1, retained dual membership with ILYM until 2007
Twin Cities (St. Paul, MN)	1948	1956	Preparative under Minneapolis as Church St. Mtg; joined ILYM 1956; NYM #1
Eau Claire-Menomonie (WI)	1956	1975	Preparative under Twin Cities; NYM #1
Duluth Superior (MN/WI)	1962	1989	Preparative Twin Cities 1970 to 1989
Beloit (WI)	1970	1978	Under care of Madison 1970–78, prior to 1970 worshipped with Rock Valley, IL meeting
Oshkosh (WI)	1970	1974	Self- identification, NYM #1 Retains membership in ILYM
Fox Valley (Green Bay, WI)	1971	1975	Green Bay Worship Group under Madison; NYM #1
Prospect Hill (St. Paul, MN)	1973	1983	Preparative Twin Cities
Bismarck (ND)	1982	1983	By self identification, NYM Clearness
Kickapoo Valley (Gays Mills, WI)	1975	1981	NYM Clearness Committee
Lake Superior (Marquette, MI)	1975	1979	Preparative under Fox Valley

Appendices

Red River (Fargo ND, Moorhead MN)	1977	1996	Preparative Twin Cities; NYM Clearness Committee
Cannon Valley	1978	1983	Preparative under Twin Cities, NYM Clearness Committee
Keweenaw (Houghton, MI)	1980	1983	Formerly Houghton Worship Group under Lake Superior, also NYM Clearness Committee
Stevens Point (WI)	1980	1997	Preparative under Eau Claire-Menomonie; NYM Clearness Committee
Brainerd (MN)	1982	1993	Preparative Duluth-Superior
St Cloud (MN)	1982	1986	Preparative under Minneapolis; NYM Clearness Committee; Laid down 1994
St Croix Valley (Stillwater, MN)	1982	1983	By self-identification; Twin Cities and NYM Clearness Committee
Eau Claire (WI)	1996	1999	Change of name from Eau Claire- Menomonie

Did not join NYM

Rock Valley Meeting, IL	before 1956	part of ILYM Northern Halfly; remained with ILYM
McHenry, IL		part of ILYM Northern Halfly; remained with ILYM

Worship Groups	Began to Meet	Description
North Central WI (Merrill)	about 1963	Preparative under Madison
Yahara (Madison, WI)	1972	inactive in NYM since 1998, now under care of Iowa Conservative
Dodgeville (WI)	1981	under care of Madison
Sand Ridge (Black Earth, WI)	1990	under care of Madison

FAITH AND PRACTICE

Platteville (WI)	1990	meets intermittently
Northfield (MN)	1958	since 1978 mostly meets with Cannon Valley
Mankato (MN)	1967	also ties to Iowa Conservative
Marshall (MN)		also ties to Iowa Conservative
Sioux Falls (SD)		
Fort Atkinson (WI)	1969	met from 1969–75, active in ILYM Northern Halfly
Decorah Friends Fellowship (IA)	1969	joined Iowa Conservative in 1995; participates in NYM Extended Driftless (regional) Gathering
Dubuque (IA)	1970	under care of Madison
Interlake (Manitowoc WI)	1972	under care of Fox Valley
La Crosse (WI)	1977	included Winona from 1984–95
Winona (MN)	1995	Preparative under Minneapolis
Bemidji (MN)	1982	met intermittently until 1990, see Northern Lights
Grand Rapids (MN)	1985	
Northern Lights (MN)	1994	includes Lake Itasca, Bemidji, under care of Duluth
Plum Creek	1996	
Viroqua (WI)	1998	Joined w/ Kickapoo Valley 2001, reformed in 2013
St Peter	1999	
Ripon/ Winnebago (WI)	1999	under care of Madison
Shawano (WI)	2000	under care of Fox Valley
Kenosha- Racine (WI)	2000	under care of Milwaukee

Appendices

Appendix E: Clerks of Northern Halfly & Yearly, 1960–2000

Clerks generally served two-year terms, clerking four annual sessions. In some instances, changes were made mid-year.

Northern Half-yearly Meeting 1960–Sept, 1975:

1960 Charles Wright
1961 Robert Greenler
1962 George Parzen
1963 Margaret Stevens
1964 Bimsy Kirkpatrick
1966 Ray Treadway
1968 Frank Wood
1969 Ralph Raymond
1971 Nathaniel Sample
1973 Howard Lutz
1974 Nancy Crom
1974 Nancy Breitsprecher
1975 Nina Gold

Northern Yearly Meeting Sept. 1975 –2016

1975 Nina Gold
1976 Stan White
1978 JoAnn Elder
1980 Howard Lutz
1982 Ellen Brooks
1984 Perry-O Sliwa
1986 John Martinson
1988 Marian Van Dellen
1990 Laura Fraser (last year with two sessions annually)
1992 Jim Greenley
1996 Mary Snyder and Frank Wood, co-clerks

Faith and Practice

1997 Marian Van Dellen
1998 Jean Eden and Lorene Ludy, co-clerks

Appendices

Appendix F: Minneapolis Meeting: A Quick Tour of the Past by Elaine Carte

1851

William Wales and family, Quakers from Indiana, settle in village of St. Anthony.

Minneapolis is established a year later on west side of Mississippi River.

1860

Small meetinghouse built at 8th St. and Hennepin Ave. Friends meet for worship on First and Fifth Days and maintain library.

> *The plain little building with its high, facing seats for the elders...a number of the women wore the plain gray dress with white kerchief and small gray bonnet...It was heated by stoves, and lighted, on the rare occasions of evening service, by kerosene lamps in wall brackets. A big old wall clock ticked out the passing time in a soothing rhythm. Families sat together, as there was no segregation of sexes.*
> —Alexina Gray

1863

Minneapolis becomes official monthly meeting affiliated with Iowa Yearly Meeting. Membership is 145 in 1870, including many farm families attending preparative meetings west of city.

> *Friends maintain a testimony against Priests and Ministers wages, and against Slavery, Lotteries, and trading in Goods taken in war. There is one instance of violation of our testimony against oaths, and two instances of assisting the military service.*
> —Minneapolis to Iowa YM, 1860s.

Faith and Practice

1864
Meeting forms Committee on Concerns of People of Color, which conducts school for several years in St. Anthony.

1880s–90s
Evangelical movement and regional prosperity bring growth to area meetings. Minneapolis lists 294 members in 1892.

1885
William Pearson becomes first paid pastor.

1893
Monthly meeting ends traditional Quaker practice of holding separate men's and women's business meetings.

1895
New meetinghouse built at 14th St. and First Ave. South.

1900s–10s
Numbers decline as rural families move to land farther west and meeting fails to draw newcomers.

> *We are isolated from any large body of Friends, and are thrown on our own resources. We must face the difficulties incident to maintaining a Friends Meeting in a Large City (these are many and great.)*
> —Minneapolis to Iowa YM, 1905.

1902
Minneapolis becomes part of Five Years Meeting, now Friends United Meeting, as it is established by Iowa and other YMs.

1909
Pastor Edward Kelsey, hired to spark meeting growth, introduces printed bulletins andother innovations.

Appendices

1917

As US prepares to enter World War I, meeting sends telegram to Woodrow Wilson opposing universal military training. Women begin gathering one day a week to sew garments for refugees in Europe. After armistice a year later, meeting minutes "unanimous feeling" that new American Friends Service Committee be continued.

Barbara Tyler Parrott, who was born into a meeting family in 1910, remembers "Aunt Edith" Jones supervising Sunday School while Ruth and Lucia Worrall served as teachers. The children sang with the help of a pump organ and recited memory verses. Gordon Coffin also attended meeting as a child in the 1920s and 1930s. At meeting for worship, "Faithful attenders tended to get 'set' in their seating. Perhaps one might be hard of hearing, or want more light (and more Light), or leave early, or sit by friends... [U]sually we sang a couple of hymns. After the collection...there was a short quiet period, and then the sermon by the minister."

1930s

Temperance work is active concern: Roscoe Coffin serves as president of Minnesota Temperance Movement, and pastors Ellison Purdy and Millard Jones preach regularly at Union City Mission. In 1942 Gordon Coffin left Minneapolis for 4 years in Civilian Public Service as a conscientious objector. Joe White, a Quaker from southern Minnesota, made the same difficult decision. Herb Crocker and Andy Gibas, who came from other religious traditions, refused military service in the 1940s and would later support choices made by their sons during the Vietnam War.

1947

Richard Newby begins 11-year pastorate that helps to revitalize meeting by bringing in new people, especially young families.

Catherine and Herb Crocker met at a CPS smoke jumpers camp in Montana during World War II. They returned to Minneapolis,

Herb's hometown, after the war and started attending his UCC church, but they felt they didn't fit it. After visiting other churches they decided to join Minneapolis Meeting in 1951. Catherine remembers that Richard Newby seemed almost "the meeting" to them. The Crockers and their children regularly attended Family Night, a time of "food and fun."

1948
Friends worship group begins meeting near University of Minnesota, eventually becoming Twin Cities Friends Meeting. In 1956, after several years as preparative meeting with Minneapolis, new monthly meeting joins Illinois YM.

1950
Meeting buys and moves into church building at York Ave. South and 44th St.

1962
Local office of AFSC opens in Twin Cities; when this office closes in 1981, Quakers continue local peace and justice work by founding Friends for a Non-Violent World.

1960s–70s
Vietnam War draws people to meeting in response to Friends' peace testimony. Several men from meeting families are conscientious objectors.

1975
Twin Cities and other monthly meetings in Illinois YM establish Northern YM in response to growth in region.

1982
Minneapolis Meeting ends its long affiliation with Iowa YM. Differences in outlook, geographical separation, and Iowa's oppo-

Appendices

sition to work of some national Quaker organizations contribute to decision.

1988
Local Friends establish Friends School of Minnesota.

1991
Minneapolis joins Northern YM, affiliate of Friends General Conference, after time of reflection during which members travel to many YMs and other Quaker gatherings.

1992
Meeting completes major remodeling of York Ave. building. First Day mornings include two worship hours—one unprogrammed, the other with planned speaking and music—and active First Day School program. Minnesota Friends extended beyond Minneapolis Friends Meeting.

Faith and Practice

Index

adult 81, 90, 91, 107, 138, 157, 159
AFSC 87, 115, 137, 147–148, 153, 154, 170, 203, 204
annual session 75, 80, 81, 86, 108, 122, 148, 150, 161
associate. *See* membership
attenders 18, 70, 74, 84, 86, 91, 95, 96, 117, 120, 156, 160, 194, 203

baptism 17
Barclay, Robert 17, 18–19, 69, 70
Bathurst, Elizabeth 2, 5
beliefs 15, 18, 22, 31, 32, 33, 44, 55, 95, 99, 109, 116, 192, 194, 213
Bible 17, 121, 129, 131, 133, 152
Birkel, Michael 35, 40
birth 79, 91, 108, 119, 189
birthright 91
Boulding, Kenneth 97, 103, 154
Brinton, Anna Cox 177
business. *See* Meeting for Business

Called Meeting for Business 77
Calvi, John 171
Camp Woodbrooke (WI) 114
Cary, Stephen 176–177
children 17, 18, 28, 42, 47, 69, 80, 84, 91, 101–103, 105–106, 107–111, 113–117, 119, 122, 135, 136, 137, 138, 162, 175, 193, 203, 204
Christ 15, 22, 29, 35, 41, 44, 130, 143, 144, 170, 171, 172
Christianity 16, 41, 133
Church of England 129
Civilian Public Service 146, 152, 153, 154, 203
clearness committee 56–58, 83, 84, 85, 92–93, 94, 98–99, 102, 104, 122
clerk 67, 73–76, 83–86, 92, 93, 94, 99, 121, 132
Coffin, Gordon 203
Coffin, Roscoe 203
communion 17, 65, 67
community 9, 11, 13, 14, 16, 18, 22, 23, 24, 26, 27, 32, 33, 34, 39, 41–42, 45, 48, 51–59, 61, 65, 66, 67, 68, 69, 71, 76, 79, 80, 81, 89, 92, 93, 94, 95, 96, 97, 98, 101, 102, 104, 105, 107–111, 113, 114, 115, 116, 124, 148, 152, 154, 159, 164, 189, 213
concerns 24, 26, 28, 52, 54, 63, 73, 79, 80, 81, 84, 93, 106, 116, 122, 148, 154, 155, 161, 189
convincement 91

Cooper, Wilmer 20
creation 21–25, 28, 38, 40, 41, 69
Crocker, Catherine and Herb 203–204
Cromwell, Oliver 35, 129
Cronk, Sandra 36, 40

death 56, 119–125, 130, 145, 174
decision making 72, 77
Deism 133
disability 120, 123
disarmament 38
discernment 14, 18, 27, 28, 32, 52, 56–59, 71, 76, 78, 80, 91, 169
dissent 73, 75–76
Divine Light 42, 152
Divine Presence 17, 53, 65–66, 69, 171
Divine Spirit 15, 58, 67, 71, 100
divorce 101, 103
Dunbar, Barrington 169, 170

Earlham School of Religion 138, 178
earth 21–30, 36, 80, 119, 173
education 90, 113–117, 123, 132, 138, 156, 161, 163
elders 61, 201
Emancipation Proclamation 135–136
epistles 44, 136
equality 18, 24, 41–45, 108, 130, 132
ESYM/El Salvador 43, 87, 140, 160–162
Evangelical Friends Church International 135, 139, 140
experiential 36

faith 14, 15, 17, 31, 32, 33, 34, 36, 42, 48, 52, 61, 65, 66, 71, 80, 91, 92, 93, 108, 110, 113, 115, 124, 127, 130, 193
FCNL 115, 137

Fell, Margaret 130, 144
Fell, Thomas 130
FGC 45, 50, 87, 115, 127, 137–139, 152, 154, 158, 175, 178, 205
finance 87, 106, 157
Firbank Fell (England) 130
First Day School. *See* education
FNVW 115
Fogelklou, Emilia 174
Fox, George 16, 18, 24, 29, 35, 40, 41, 44, 51, 54, 59, 71, 72, 78, 79, 88, 114, 129–131, 132, 136, 141, 143–144, 145, 149, 175
Friendly Folk Dancers 157–159
FUM 138, 139, 154, 196
funerals 120, 124
FWCC 87, 139–141, 147–148, 150, 158, 160–161

gathered meeting 52–53, 66, 67, 70
Gibas, Andy 203
gift 23, 36, 43, 52, 102, 121
God 15, 16, 17, 18, 20, 21, 22, 23, 24, 25, 28, 31, 35, 36, 37, 38, 39, 41, 43, 44, 47, 51, 52, 65, 66, 67, 68, 69, 71, 72, 73, 75, 76, 77, 78, 79, 80, 97, 98, 100, 102, 103, 105, 107, 113, 114, 119, 131, 132, 143, 155, 159, 169, 173, 174, 175, 179, 192, 193, 213
Gould, Lisa 22, 29
Great Revival 151–152
Gurneyite 134, 136–137
Gurney, Joseph John 134
Gwyn, Douglas 127

Harnden, Philip 170
Havens, Joseph 154
Hicks, Elias 133–134
Hicksite 134, 136, 137, 138–139

Index

history 16, 17, 23, 56, 58, 92, 113, 116, 117, 127, 137, 138, 145, 147, 148, 159, 165
Hole, Francis 5, 163, 172–173
Hutchinson, Hannah 2, 5

Illinois Yearly Meeting 138, 139, 152, 153, 154, 155, 156, 157, 164
Inner Guide 32, 163
Inner Light 133
integrity 18, 20, 24, 27, 31–34, 108, 132
intervisitation 53, 161
Iowa Yearly Meeting 114, 151–152, 154, 160, 201

Jesus 23, 29, 36, 41, 44, 61, 130, 162
Johnson, Eric W. 177
Jones, Edith H. 163, 203
Jones, Millard 203
Jones, Rufus 107, 110, 136–138, 150, 153, 175, 176–177
justice 38, 39, 137, 141, 149, 204

Kelly, Thomas R. 47, 49, 66, 70
Kelsey, Edward 202
King Charles II 143–145
Kraft, John 5, 175
Kriebel, Ann 171

Langworthy, David 5, 171–172
leadings 16, 17, 18, 20, 27, 31, 33, 42, 52, 54, 55, 56, 65, 72, 89–90, 109, 132
Light 15, 16, 27, 28, 39, 41, 42, 43, 51, 58, 66, 67, 71, 73, 79, 101, 102, 133, 152, 169, 171, 203
listening 16, 52–53, 56, 57, 58, 66, 67, 68, 74, 108, 110, 163, 193
Love 41, 42, 43, 103, 172

Madison Monthly Meeting 110, 152–153, 163, 165
marriage 56–57, 97–106, 194, 195
McCutchan, Alden 26, 30
Meeting for Business 73, 77, 156, 190–191
Meeting for Worship 41, 65, 67, 68, 73, 121, 177, 178
membership 13, 51, 56, 63, 81, 84, 85, 89–96, 124, 132, 133, 139, 153, 154, 156, 190, 194, 196
  becoming a member 91–93
  definition of 89–90
  recording of 90
  termination of 94–95
  transfer of 93–94
Milwaukee Monthly Meeting 152, 153, 154, 156, 158, 163, 196, 198
ministry 42, 56, 67, 68, 69, 90, 140, 158, 159
Minneapolis Monthly Meeting 104, 151, 153, 154, 156, 159–160, 161, 163, 165, 196, 197, 198, 201, 202, 203, 204, 205
minute 24, 73, 79, 98, 122, 124, 150, 156, 164
monthly meeting 57, 81, 82, 83, 84, 85, 89, 90, 91, 93, 94, 95, 96, 98, 101, 125, 152, 153, 154, 164, 196, 201, 204
Mott, Lucretia Coffin 97, 103, 135, 176
Muggletonians 129
Mullen, Tom 178
mysticism 137, 138

Newby, Richard 203–204
Nightingales 157, 158, 178–179
Nobel Peace Prize 137, 148
Northern Yearly Meeting 14, 15, 22,

209

24, 26, 29, 30, 43, 45, 54, 55,
67, 79–88, 90, 91, 97, 98, 103,
104, 108, 110, 114–115, 139,
140, 148, 150, 151, 155–165,
175, 176, 177, 178, 189–191,
192–194, 196–198, 199–200,
213

oaths 131, 201
obedience 15, 80, 175
officers 83, 84, 86, 131
orthodox 133
outreach 157

Parrott, Barbara Tyler 203
pastoral 56, 63, 151, 160, 178
peace 18, 24, 35–40, 47, 54, 65, 108,
115, 132, 135, 137, 152, 154,
155, 158, 159, 204
peace witness 143–150
Pearson, William 202
Pendle Hill (England) 130
Penn, Admiral William 131
Penn, William 21, 29, 41, 45, 69, 70,
103, 114, 119, 125, 131, 136,
145–146
Pennington, Issac 54, 59
Perez, Raul 43, 45
Peterson, Diane J. 25, 29
Peterson, Nancy 5, 9, 61
poverty 36, 171, 176
prayer 17, 66, 107, 120, 159, 171
preparative meeting 81, 82, 83, 85,
92, 95–96, 153, 154, 164, 204
presence 15, 17, 22, 52–53, 56, 65, 66,
67, 69, 90, 100, 105, 107, 108,
148, 163, 171, 172, 195
programmed Friends 16, 121
Purdy, Ellison 203
Puritans 129

quarterly meetings 151
queries 13–14, 57, 104
Quietism 131–133

Ranters 129
Religious Society of Friends 20,
29, 30, 73, 79, 82, 88, 89–90,
91–92, 94, 95, 96, 103, 116,
117, 129, 137, 140, 143, 150,
163, 169, 189, 194, 195
Right Sharing of World Resources
115
Roman Catholic 129
Rowell, Teresina 154

St. Paul, MN. *See* Twin Cities Friends
Scattergood School 87, 114
seasoning. *See* decision making
semi-programmed Friends 16, 67
sense of the meeting 52–53, 73,
75–76, 80, 194
Shacter, Ellie 172–173
silence 65, 67, 68, 131
simplicity 5, 7, 47, 49, 50, 171
Smith, Steve 171
sojourners 94
Spann, Niyonu D. 44, 45
spirit 15–17, 20, 22, 27, 28, 31, 32, 42,
43, 44, 51–53, 56, 58, 61, 65,
66, 67, 68, 69, 71, 72, 74, 75,
77, 80, 89–90, 100, 104, 108,
109, 110, 113, 114, 117, 132,
139, 143–144, 145, 159, 170,
171, 175, 178, 193, 194
spiritual nurture 52, 109, 148, 157,
159, 162, 178
spoken ministry 68, 90
Steere, Douglas 154
Stephen, Caroline 65, 70
stewardship 24, 122

Index

Taber, Frances I. 5, 48–49, 50
teens 107, 110
termination. *See* membership
testimonies 16, 17, 18, 20, 24, 26,
    35–36, 37, 38, 39, 40, 41, 43,
    44, 47–49, 48, 49, 52, 80, 89,
    95, 99, 108, 120, 122, 132, 135,
    143, 144, 145, 146, 147, 148,
    201, 204, 211
Thomas, Sheila 5, 31, 34
threshing 75–76
transfer. *See* membership
traveling. *See* intervisitation
Truth 5, 17, 20, 29, 32, 33, 42, 44, 52,
    61, 68, 69, 71, 72, 75, 76, 77,
    90, 98, 113, 114, 116, 144, 171
Twin Cities Friends 29, 97, 98, 103,
    154, 161, 163, 204

unity 15, 22, 27–28, 34, 52, 71, 74,
    75–77, 80, 137, 138, 144
unprogrammed Friends 16, 67, 121,
    152, 178, 205

Van Dellen, Rich 178, 179
violence 35, 36, 37, 39, 146–147, 148,
    174
vocal ministry 68, 69

Wahl, Rosalie 5, 80, 88, 165, 178
Wales, William 201
war 25, 35–40, 129, 133, 135, 137,
    144, 145–149, 150, 152,
    153, 154, 170, 171, 174, 201,
    203–204
Watson, Elizabeth 169
wedding 99–101, 102, 103, 105
Weerts, Patty 5, 31, 34

White, Joe 203
Whittier, John Greenleaf 119, 125,
    179
Wilbur, John 134
Wilson., E. Raymond 154
Wilson, Woodrow 203
witness 9, 11, 26, 28, 35, 36, 37, 39,
    41, 43, 47, 48, 81, 115, 144,
    145, 148, 152, 159
Wood, Raquel 5, 163, 177–178
Woolman, John 16, 18, 21, 25, 29,
    42, 45, 132–133, 145, 149, 174,
    175, 176
Worrall, Lucia 203
Worrall, Ruth 203
worship 11, 13, 16, 17, 41, 42, 43, 51,
    52, 53, 54, 55, 57, 63, 65–70,
    71, 72, 73, 74, 75, 76, 77, 80,
    81, 82, 83, 84, 85, 90, 92, 93,
    94, 95, 96, 98, 99, 100, 101,
    107–108, 109, 110, 114, 120,
    121–122, 123, 124, 129, 131,
    134, 136, 139, 152, 153, 154,
    156, 157, 158, 159, 161, 163,
    176, 190, 194, 201, 203, 204,
    205
worship group 57, 81, 82–83, 85, 92,
    95, 96, 139, 153, 154, 190, 204

yearly meeting 9, 13, 53, 75, 79, 81,
    85, 89, 95, 96, 98, 115, 134,
    136, 138, 140, 148, 151, 152,
    156, 158, 159, 160, 161, 162,
    189, 192, 193
Young, Mildred Binns 51, 59
youth 40, 80, 110, 114, 157, 161, 162

Zarembka, David 174–175

FAITH AND PRACTICE

This Faith and Practice, developed over a period of twenty-two years, reminds us of our ways of being and acting together in Northern Yearly Meeting. It teaches people who join with us about our beliefs and how we act to carry out God's ways in the upper Midwest. It helps readers within our midst and beyond our community to understand our religion—who we are, what we cherish, and how and why we practice Quakerism.

www.ingramcontent.com/pod-product-compliance
Lightning Source LLC
Chambersburg PA
CBHW021848090426

42811CB00033B/2185/J